**New Directions for
Community Colleges**

Arthur M. Cohen
EDITOR-IN-CHIEF

Caroline Q. Durdella
Nathan R. Durdella
ASSOCIATE EDITORS

WITHDRAWN

Strengthening Community Colleges Through Institutional Collaborations

Michael J. Roggow

EDITOR

Number 165 • Spring 2014
Jossey-Bass
San Francisco

STRENGTHENING COMMUNITY COLLEGES THROUGH INSTITUTIONAL COLLABORATIONS
Michael J. Roggow (ed.)
New Directions for Community Colleges, no. 165

Arthur M. Cohen, Editor-in-Chief
Caroline Q. Durdella, Nathan R. Durdella, Associate Editors

NEW DIRECTIONS FOR COMMUNITY COLLEGES (ISSN 0194-3081, electronic ISSN 1536-0733) is part of The Jossey-Bass Higher and Adult Education Series and is published quarterly by Wiley Subscription Services, Inc., A Wiley Company, at Jossey-Bass, One Montgomery St., Ste. 1200, San Francisco, CA 94104. POSTMASTER: Send address changes to New Directions for Community Colleges, Jossey-Bass, One Montgomery St., Ste. 1200, San Francisco, CA 94104.

SUBSCRIPTIONS cost $89 for individuals in the U.S., Canada, and Mexico, and $113 in the rest of the world for print only; $89 in all regions for electronic only; $98 in the U.S., Canada, and Mexico for combined print and electronic; $122 for combined print and electronic in the rest of the world. Institutional print only subscriptions are $311 in the U.S., $351 in Canada and Mexico, and $385 in the rest of the world; electronic only subscriptions are $311 in all regions; combined print and electronic subscriptions are $357 in the U.S., $397 in Canada and Mexico, and $431 in the rest of the world.

EDITORIAL CORRESPONDENCE should be sent to the Editor-in-Chief, Arthur M. Cohen, at 1749 Mandeville Lane, Los Angeles, CA 90049. All manuscripts receive anonymous reviews by external referees.

New Directions for Community Colleges is indexed in CIJE: Current Index to Journals in Education (ERIC), Contents Pages in Education (T&F), Current Abstracts (EBSCO), Ed/Net (Simpson Communications), Education Index/Abstracts (H. W. Wilson), Educational Research Abstracts Online (T&F), ERIC Database (Education Resources Information Center), and Resources in Education (ERIC).

Microfilm copies of issues and articles are available in 16mm and 35mm, as well as microfiche in 105mm, through University Microfilms Inc., 300 North Zeeb Road, Ann Arbor, MI 48106-1346.

CONTENTS

EDITOR'S NOTES   1
Michael J. Roggow

FOREWORD   5
Kevin E. Drumm

1. College to High School: Kentucky's Dual Enrollment   7
Alternative
Lisa G. Stephenson
This chapter illustrates the impact two dual enrollment programs have
on high school students in a rural area by enabling them to take college-
level courses at local community colleges.

2. The Role of Secondary School and Community College   17
Collaborations to Increase Latinas in Engineering in a Rural
Community
Soko S. Starobin, Glennda M. Bivens
This chapter shares insights from a case study about the impact
one Latina counselor has on exposing rural Latina students to pre-
engineering programs, and how institutional collaborations can in-
crease participation among Latinas in engineering.

3. Improving Student Performance Outcomes and Graduation   25
Rates Through Institutional Partnerships
Michael J. Roggow
In this chapter, the author describes useful strategies for improving student learning and performance outcomes, and how new approaches to
teaching and advisement can increase college graduation and transfer
rates for minority students.

4. Collaborating for Social Justice Through Service Learning   37
Tom DePaola
This chapter provides critical evidence about how the service learning
program at an urban community college helps students support the
development of academic knowledge and skills, while helping them
understand the importance of civic engagement.

5. Turning Knowledge Into Success: The Role of Collaboration   49
in Knowledge Management Implementation
Handan Hizmetli
In this chapter, the author shares valuable insights and recommendations for building a knowledge-management-oriented campus environment that can inform effective strategic planning.

6. Student Affairs and Information Technology: Collaborating   59
in the Cloud
Peter Reyes Barbatis
In this chapter, the author discusses how student affairs and institutional technology departments can work together to improve satisfaction among new students as they navigate the college admissions process.

7. The Role of Key Administrators in Internationalizing the   67
Community College Student Experience
Ronald D. Opp, Penny Poplin Gosetti
In this chapter, the authors argue that a range of key administrators and faculty should be involved in helping to generate student interest in study abroad and in infusing global perspectives across community college curricula.

8. Collaboration: Use of Consortia to Promote International   77
Education
Rosalind Latiner Raby, Donald R. Culton, Edward J. Valeau
This chapter provides a historical overview and discourse about advancing the international education agenda thorough the use of consortia and partnerships to accelerate knowledge among college students about global topics.

9. Collaborations Between the State and Local Colleges: 87
Sleeping With the Enemy?
Elizabeth Cox Brand
In this chapter, the author introduces us to the ingredients of successful partnerships between a centralized state-level department and local community colleges.

INDEX   95

Editor's Notes

Among centers of higher education, community colleges are often at the vanguard of institutional collaboration. With so many agendas—responding to needs of local communities, preparing students for the workplace, soliciting funds to strengthen resources, and preparing students for the transition to four-year colleges and universities and the pursuit of their baccalaureate degrees—institutional success is often a function of organized, long-range, and cooperative relationships within and among these institutions.

Presidential visions, economic conditions, community needs, and student demographics can shape collaboration among community colleges. Designed to strengthen educational pipelines, academic departments at two-year institutions often work interdependently to bridge secondary education, associate, and baccalaureate programs. These cross-sector collaborations address issues on a vertical as well as horizontal level.

Continuously changing student demographics, technology, global economic demands, and business models have forced community colleges to develop partnerships never before conceived. These partnerships have been shown to correlate with improved student performance outcomes, retention, and financial stability.

Authored by community college leaders and researchers who continue to shape their institutional successes through research and collaborative practice, this proposed volume of *New Directions for Community Colleges* provides insight into the wide array of collaborations.

The journal is divided into four parts. The first part (Chapters 1–4) highlights partnerships that bring together secondary and postsecondary institutions, collaborations among college divisions and departments, and grant-supported methods for teaching and engaging students from underrepresented backgrounds. The second part focuses on ways institutional technology partners with academic and student affairs departments to improve student satisfaction and teaching and learning, and student retention. Part three explores the critical need for students to become more globally aware, and the inter- and intrainstitutional partnerships required to make this a priority. Finally, the fourth part describes how a state education department works with individual community colleges in the state.

Inspiring high school students to earn a college degree can be difficult, especially for minority and other underrepresented students. Partnerships between middle schools, high schools, and community colleges, as well as support from communities, can often work together to motivate students to attend college. The first two chapters focus on providing venues for underrepresented students, including women, to attend college in rural areas of the Midwest and South. In the first chapter, Lisa G. Stephenson

New Directions for Community Colleges, no. 165, Spring 2014 © 2014 Wiley Periodicals, Inc.
Published online in Wiley Online Library (wileyonlinelibrary.com) • DOI: 10.1002/cc.20084

illustrates the impact two grant-funded, dual-enrollment programs in Kentucky have on high school students by enabling them to take college-level courses at local community colleges. In Chapter 2, Soko S. Starobin and Glennda M. Bivens illustrate the impact one Latina counselor has on exposing rural Latina students to pre-engineering programs. It also shares new insights about how intersections of race, gender, and language can strengthen institutional collaborations to increase participation among Latinas in engineering.

In Chapter 3, I tell the story of how an urban community college and a four-year college in New York City received a large federal grant award to increase college graduation and transfer rates for minority students. A new criminal justice program at the community college provides a venue for experimenting with new tools and methods for effective teaching, advising, and tutoring. Federal grant funds paved the way for this project, which was organized by several faculty committed to working together. This chapter shares several recommendations for securing grant funding to implement new methods for program development, improving student learning and performance outcomes, and advising for a range of first-generation college students.

In Chapter 4, Tom DePaola provides critical evidence about how a service learning program at an urban community college helps students reflect and synthesize internship experiences with academic knowledge and skills, while helping them understand the importance of civic engagement. He highlights the stories of two students from diverse backgrounds whose internship experiences helped them integrate both action and reflection through service learning pedagogy. He provides unique insights about how developing partnerships between community colleges and local internship sites are an important responsibility of community colleges, as they encourage students to better understand social issues that impact their communities and help them make informed decisions about their career paths.

Certain departments on community college campuses—for example, the institutional research office—do not typically come to mind when we think about college life, but they are among the most important. Institutional Research and Planning is one of them, and as Handan Hizmetli illustrates in Chapter 5, an effective institutional research office not only collects data for institutional analysis but also provides knowledge in usable and understandable ways to help administrators and faculty make informed strategic decisions that critically impact their institutions. Hizmetli points out the urgency for a certain urban community college to improve its student performance outcomes, which it did by piloting an innovative freshman year seminar. Early on, the seminar yielded promising results, improving student grades and retention rates. This initiative would not have been successful without collaboration among nearly all divisions across the campus and the sharing of valuable information through a knowledge management model. Hizmetli shares valuable insights and recommendations for building a knowledge-management-oriented campus environment.

In an era of declining student enrollments and competition among colleges, Peter Reyes Barbatis meets the needs of digitally savvy students by introducing ways to improve student satisfaction and retention rates using effective technologically based tools that require partnership between enrollment management and information technology. In Chapter 6, Barbatis discusses how the use of these tools increases student satisfaction, particularly for new students who often run the risk of getting lost in the admissions process. He introduces best practices and future initiatives, including the admissions pipeline, smart-device applications, customized educational planning, and financial aid program compliance—all of which can help colleges more effectively plan to accommodate new students.

Promoting global perspectives across curricula and expanding students' awareness about international topics are critical to any curricula in higher education. Student recognition of and appreciation for global learning are often included in community college general education-based proficiencies and are often acknowledged by outside reviewers when academic programs undergo assessment. Funding these programs can be challenging for many institutions, but the national agenda to promote global learning is here to stay. In Chapter 7, Ronald D. Opp and Penny Poplin Gosetti argue that a range of key administrators and faculty should be involved in helping to generate student interest in study abroad and in infusing global perspectives across community college curricula. Resources should also be used to support international students and to socially integrate domestic and international students. To develop a culture of internationalization, the authors suggest that boards of trustees and the president should become personally involved, alongside administrators, faculty, and students.

In Chapter 8, Rosalind Latiner Raby, Donald R. Culton, and Edward J. Valeau further advance the international education agenda by describing collaboration through the lens of using a nonprofit consortium, the California Colleges for International Education (CCIE), to promote international education. CCIE facilitates faculty internationalization of classroom instruction and expands education abroad and international student programming. This organization provides practitioners with examples of collaboration involving personal communication and networking, and pooling human and financial resources, to accelerate knowledge among college students about global topics.

In an era of diminishing resources and a growing demand for accountability, Elizabeth Cox Brand introduces us, in Chapter 9, to the ingredients of successful partnerships between a greatly centralized state-level department and local community colleges in Oregon that exist under it. The author argues for strong leadership, communication, trust, and shared vision as foundations for sustaining productive partnerships that fuel state funding to local campuses and recommends strategies for successful collaboration in highly politicized educational environments.

Michael J. Roggow
Editor

MICHAEL J. ROGGOW is director of the Criminal Justice Program at City University of New York's Bronx Community College. He is also an adjunct assistant professor of psychology.

NEW DIRECTIONS FOR COMMUNITY COLLEGES • DOI: 10.1002/cc

Foreword

Kevin E. Drumm

In an era of declining student enrollments, state budget cuts, and shifting student demographics, successful institutional partnerships are timely and necessary. College presidents often initiate them, and faculty and administrators build and sustain them. Healthy, productive efforts to partner often yield immediate benefits for students, and longer range collaborative planning has strengthened and will continue to strengthen institutions for years. This volume of *New Directions for Community Colleges* paints a lively portrait of partnerships that fuel student learning and advance the growth of a range of rural and urban community colleges. As the president of the State University of New York's Broome Community College (SUNY Broome), I am delighted to introduce this volume capturing examples of well-orchestrated institutional collaborations.

In recent years, I have seen many community colleges across the United States and abroad work together in creative and sustainable ways in support of innovative pedagogy and student services. At my own college in the last few years, we have built local, regional, statewide, and global partnerships, which have already shown significant and measurable outcomes. Successful partnerships are doable and necessary. My own college is located in an area of New York State where shrinking demographics signifies challenges we face every day. At one point, our revenue base was mostly student enrollment driven. As this is no longer the case, we must constantly think about ways to forge regional, national, and international partnerships to promote an educated and talented workforce.

Once thought of as primarily serving the communities where they're located, community colleges now must think more broadly about their scope of service. We now rely on them to address a broader range of economic needs outside those in their immediate locales. This is especially true in areas of the United States where once prosperous manufacturing communities have gradually declined or disappeared. The economy of Binghamton, New York, where my institution is located, for example, continues to contract, especially after two major companies that fueled our local economy were forced to downsize due to U.S. and international economic market conditions.

The collection of chapters in this volume represents the work of various faculty, administrators, and other professionals who discovered ways to successfully advance their institutions using collaborative approaches. Their topics will generate awareness about student trends and issues, which

NEW DIRECTIONS FOR COMMUNITY COLLEGES, no. 165, Spring 2014 © 2014 Wiley Periodicals, Inc.
Published online in Wiley Online Library (wileyonlinelibrary.com) • DOI: 10.1002/cc.20085

are intended to help us reach for ways to sustain and enhance college operating budgets during these precarious economic times. They help us think strategically about securing grant funds to address institutional challenges; retaining students through good teaching and student support services; and capitalizing on dual enrollment, STEM, and study abroad programs. They illustrate effective collaborations with institutional research and ways for enrollment management and institutional technology to work together to improve student satisfaction, especially among new students.

This volume also offers insights about how community colleges can work effectively with state education departments toward meeting shared goals. As I familiarize myself with them, I am reminded of some similar kinds of partnerships that now exist on my own campus, details of which I will share. As you move through these chapters, new tools for progress may catch your eye. They include ways to collaborate to strengthen educational pipelines, fuel local and statewide industry, secure outside funding to advance teaching and student services, and promote global education and workforce development. This collection of readings begins by examining academic programs designed to recruit and encourage high school students to attend college.

KEVIN E. DRUMM *is the president of SUNY Broome Community College in Binghamton, NY.*

NEW DIRECTIONS FOR COMMUNITY COLLEGES • DOI: 10.1002/cc

1

This chapter provides an overview of results from a recent qualitative study of two Middle College High Schools in Kentucky. The qualitative study utilized Rapid Assessment Process to identify essential elements needed to implement and maintain educational partnerships.

College to High School: Kentucky's Dual Enrollment Alternative

Lisa G. Stephenson

The Kentucky Postsecondary Education Improvement Act of 1997 not only created the Kentucky Community and Technical College System (KCTCS) but also charged community colleges with leading the efforts in providing education opportunities to underrepresented and underprepared populations. Dual-credit programs are just one way to expand educational opportunities in Kentucky. KCTCS dual-credit programs have traditionally included offering courses on a secondary education campus or allowing high school students to take coursework on the college campus. However, this changed with the creation of two Middle College High School (MCHS) programs at two KCTCS colleges.

As other KCTCS colleges and other postsecondary education institutions explore creating similar programs on their campuses, it is important to determine key elements necessary to create and sustain these collaborative partnerships. Findings from this study provide a framework for implementing and sustaining institutional partnerships and guidance to those considering similar endeavors.

Kentucky Middle College High Schools

In August 2009, Bluegrass Community and Technical College (BCTC) launched Opportunity Middle College (referred to hereafter as Bluegrass). BCTC has six campuses serving a diverse population of 14,000 students; its largest two are located in Lexington. Bluegrass is located on Leestown campus, the smaller of its two major campuses. The majority of courses offered on this campus are in technical program areas. Opening in the fall 2009 semester with 44 students, Bluegrass ended its first year in May 2010

NEW DIRECTIONS FOR COMMUNITY COLLEGES, no. 165, Spring 2014 © 2014 Wiley Periodicals, Inc.
Published online in Wiley Online Library (wileyonlinelibrary.com) • DOI: 10.1002/cc.20086

with 40 students. During the fall 2010 semester, there were 63 students in the program; 33 seniors and 29 juniors were enrolled in the spring 2011 semester.

The main campus of West Kentucky Community and Technical College (WKCTC) is located in Paducah, a rural western community along the Mississippi River, and serves approximately 7,500 students. Commonwealth Middle College (referred to hereafter as West Kentucky) is housed on the college's main campus. Fifty juniors were accepted into the West Kentucky program in the fall 2009 semester; all remained enrolled in the program through their graduations in May 2011. An additional 50 juniors were selected for being in the fall 2010 semester.

Bluegrass is a partnership between one P–12 school district, Fayette County Public Schools (Fayette County), and the community college, whereas West Kentucky's partnership involves the community college, two P–12 school districts, the college's foundation, and a private foundation. The P–12 school districts involved in the West Kentucky partnership are Marshall County Public Schools (Marshall County) and McCracken County Public Schools (McCracken County).

Both programs were funded to a great extent by grants. The Bluegrass program utilized a federal grant with the community college charging one half the regular tuition rate for college coursework, resulting in tuition for a three-credit hour course costing $187.50 or $195 depending on whether the student was a junior or a senior. Assessing tuition in this manner required the college to waive one half the regular tuition with the grant covering the remaining tuition balance for the students. West Kentucky is supported by a private grant and the Paducah Junior College Foundation as well as financial support from the P–12 school districts. The Support Education Excellence in Kentucky (SEEK) funding program is a formula-driven allocation through which the state distributes tax dollars to each local school. The P–12 districts who send high school students to West Kentucky forwarded their SEEK funding for each participating student to the college to support the program. This funding resulted in $3,630 to $3,838 per student, depending on P–12 school district and year, available to support the West Kentucky program. Another notable difference between the two programs is that WKCTC waives full tuition charges up to nine credit hours for college coursework; thus, tuition waived could be as much as $1,170 per MCHS student.

According to the programs' grant applications and MOUs, both Bluegrass and West Kentucky have statements that address completing a high school diploma, preparing students for college coursework, increasing student transition to college, and completion of a college credential (certificate, diploma, or degree), reducing the time to credential completion, reducing the cost of a college credential, and creating a trained workforce. Both Bluegrass and West Kentucky established student-selection criteria and hired a principal, secondary education faculty, and guidance counselors—all certified by the Kentucky Education Professional Standards Board. All salary expenses for the Bluegrass's staff were covered by the grant. SEEK and grant funds covered salaries for West Kentucky's principal and faculty; the host community college paid the salary for the guidance counselor. Fayette County served as the fiscal agent for Bluegrass, while McCracken County served as the fiscal agent for West Kentucky. The community colleges supporting these programs provide and maintain classroom and office space as well as providing some office equipment.

The setting for each program is unique. Very little remodeling was done to accommodate Bluegrass, which is located in a building also used by the carpentry program. In contrast, West Kentucky was located in a totally remodeled building on the main campus dedicated solely for the MCHS. Students in both programs complete high school graduation requirements as well as college courses. The structure of a MCHS student's day at Bluegrass differs significantly from the structure of a West Kentucky student's. High school courses at Bluegrass were offered in an independent-study model, which means that Bluegrass students took college courses any time during the day and completed their high school coursework when not in college courses. West Kentucky students completed college coursework during the morning hours while completing their high school coursework in the afternoon.

Both Bluegrass and West Kentucky students were transported by bus from their feeder high school to the college campus. Costs for transporting Bluegrass students were covered by the grant that Fayette County had received. Marshall County and McCracken County covered transportation expenses for their students attending West Kentucky. Students at both sites are provided with laptop computers. The federal grant paid for Bluegrass students' computers, and McCracken County provided laptop computers to all their high school students, so this was not an additional cost for that partnering district. However, Marshall County does not supply laptop computers for its students; the district had to purchase laptops for students participating in the West Kentucky MCHS.

Institutional Partnerships

Educational partnerships are complex and constantly changing (Amey, Eddy, & Campbell, 2010), making it difficult to create a one-size fits-all model to use when creating a partnership. The literature on these partnerships is limited with much of the available research focused on the partnerships created to provide dual-credit opportunities for high school students and transfer opportunities for community college students (Amey et al., 2010; Sink & Jackson, 2002). As community colleges seek to expand their partnerships with P–12 school districts, it is important for those involved to understand the elements of the partnership in order for it to be effective and sustained.

NEW DIRECTIONS FOR COMMUNITY COLLEGES • DOI: 10.1002/cc

Collaborative partnerships in education create seamless pathways, increase access, reduce redundancy of coursework, and allow better management of resources (Bragg, Kim, & Barnett, 2006). Recognizing that organizations wishing to collaborate needed assistance, Mattessich, Murray-Close, and Monsey (2001) identified communication, purpose, process and structure, environment, membership, and resources as the six common elements contributing to the success and longevity of the examined partnerships.

Taking a step further, Amey, Eddy, and Ozaki (2007) provide community colleges with a model that enables them to examine partnerships. These researchers argue that even though organizations who partner do receive benefits from the partnership, "many partnerships fail to obtain desired results, cannot be sustained, or cease to benefit both parties" (p. 8). While the partnership development model does not provide step-by-step instructions, it does provide partners with a way to assess the partnership from beginning through sustainability or termination.

Recognizing the limited research relating to community college partnerships, Sink and Jackson (2002) conducted a qualitative study on a community college's partnerships. Their research revealed components important to community college partnerships should include a reason to partner, a positive environment, a shared vision, and recognition of college being a leader in the community with partners understanding, respecting, and trusting each other.

While most partnerships have one leader, educational partnerships most often have a leader from each entity involved in the partnership (Cunningham & Wagonlander, 2000) with these leaders guiding, organizing, and championing partnership efforts. Champions sponsor and support the partnership (Amey et al., 2007). Champions do not necessarily need to be in a position of power or authority, but do need the support of the partnership leader.

Research Methods

Since the Bluegrass and West Kentucky MCHS programs were new and had never been studied and since limited research is available on institutional partnerships involving community colleges and P–12 school districts, a qualitative research design was appropriate to identify and describe the key elements present when these partnerships were implemented and that are perceived by key informants as necessary for the maintenance of these partnerships (Creswell, 2009). This study was conducted during the implementation period, defined as the year prior to classwork beginning through December 2011. This study utilized a survey, individual interviews, and document reviews. It is important to note that this research project is part of a companion dissertation completed by Blankenship, Bolt, Mayo, and Stephenson (2012). The dissertation team was composed of four KCTCS practitioners from diverse units within their respective colleges. In addition to research on institutional partnerships, the companion dissertation includes findings about student academic achievement, student academic engagement, and student support services in Kentucky's first two MCHSs.

This study used the concepts and practices of Rapid Assessment Process (RAP; Beebe, 2001), a team-based qualitative research method used when seeking to understand a phenomenon. RAP is an appropriate approach for conducting research when a topic needs to be explored, when research questions begin with *How* or *What*, when a detailed view of the situation is needed, and when individuals need to be studied in their natural setting. RAP allows the data-collection process to evolve while phenomena are studied in their natural settings and while the research team is developing a detailed view of the study site. The other researchers involved in the companion dissertation assisted with individual interviews, document review, and data analysis. In turn, I assisted them with their respective research studies on these programs.

The first research activity was review of the respective program grants, agendas and minutes of advisory board meetings, promotional materials, newsletters and news articles, a videotape, partners' websites, and the partnership MOUs. Individuals associated with the partnerships (i.e., grant writers, the director, academic vice president) were contacted via electronic mail if clarification was needed.

Using literature about institutional partnerships and information found through document reviews, an online survey about organizational partnerships was created and administered to both P–12 and postsecondary partners who were directly involved in the creation of Bluegrass and West Kentucky. This survey was not pilot tested because there was not a group of individuals working in other Kentucky community colleges or P–12 school districts available to pilot test the survey prior to its administration. The 29 participants who were sent the partnership survey included (a) three P–12 school district superintendents, (b) four P–12 assistant superintendents, (c) two P–12 finance directors, (d) nine high school principals, (e) two college presidents, (f) Director of Secondary Transition Initiatives, (g) two grant writers, (h) three chairs of secondary school district boards, (i) two chairs of the colleges' board of directors, and (j) one foundation chair.

The online survey included open- and closed-ended questions and a Likert-type scale allowing participants to indicate their level of agreement or disagreement concerning elements of institutional partnerships. Of the 29 individuals sent an e-mail invitation to participate in the survey research, 16 submitted responses, generating at a 55% response rate. Survey respondents included individuals affiliated with both MCHS programs: Bluegrass ($n = 5$) and West Kentucky ($n = 11$). Among the 16 survey respondents were 11 representatives of P–12 school districts and five community college partner representatives.

Eight representatives from the partnerships participated in individual interviews. Interviewees included the two college presidents and the three P–12 school district superintendents. Others interviewed were two feeder high school principals and one community college Director of Secondary Transition Initiatives (hereafter referred to as director).

While an initial set of interview questions had been approved for use in the study, the final interview questions emerged as the study progressed. The semistructured interviews included open-ended questions that allowed the interviewees to clarify or explain their responses and to discuss or summarize their role in the institutional partnerships.

While this study provides valuable information concerning the elements that contribute to the creation and implementation of institutional partnerships, the results do not provide longitudinal data. Since this study utilized qualitative strategies and involved two purposefully selected sites, findings cannot be generalized to other community colleges and P–12 school districts. However, because of site similarities, findings can assist other KCTCS colleges and other education institutions in Kentucky seeking to establish these types of programs. An additional limitation is the imbalance of survey respondents. More respondents associated with West Kentucky's program participated in the online survey than those associated with Bluegrass.

Findings

This study was an investigation of the elements necessary for implementing and maintaining collaborative educational partnerships of this nature. While the programs had similarities, there were some notable differences.

A researcher assumption at the beginning of the study was that the availability of grant funding would have the most impact on partners' decision to create the MCHSs; however, survey results indicated that providing students with the ability to start postsecondary education early and support of the P–12 school district had a greater impact on partners' decisions to create these programs than funding availability. Because all P–12 school districts involved in these two partnerships provided transportation for their students to the community college campus, a second researcher assumption was that proximity of the feeder high school to the college would be rated higher than other items; this element ranked in the top five items, but not first. A third researcher assumption was that support from P–12 school districts and support from the college board of directors would rank similarly; again, this was not the case. Support by the local community was an important consideration by those considering partnering to create an MCHS program.

Partners recognized that they were providing students with an opportunity to begin their college education at little or no cost to them or their parents. Partners expressed a shared vision—helping students be successful. College presidents shared that their respective programs were "creating access to college," "creating opportunities for student success," and "increasing contact with high schools partners and students less likely to transition to college." Interviewed superintendents shared similar comments with one sharing, ". . . this program is a vehicle to help kids go to college and explore career options." One principal shared that students who might not have considered college an option "can experience it first-hand and early without the fear of cost."

During individual interviews, noticeable differences in communication became apparent. Bluegrass had one main point of contact and communication—the director. The director communicated with MCHS personnel, Fayette County staff, the college academic unit, and the college leadership team. When discussing communication with Bluegrass personnel, there was no mention of including feeder high school principals in this process. At the time of this study, Bluegrass's advisory board was not active. In contrast, West Kentucky maintained ongoing communication through scheduled advisory board meetings with superintendents sharing information with feeder high school principals. Principals did not attend advisory meetings.

Partners believe communication has been open and honest. They recognize the need to evaluate the communication process and understand that communication is an ongoing, evolving process. The college presidents indicated that relationships were important to open and honest communication, while the superintendents agreed that communication was open and honest and that, when needed, partners communicated to resolve any issues. The principals' comments supported those made by others, but they also noted that communication had improved over time. One principal suggested that the feeder high school principals be invited to advisory committee meetings and be added to the distribution list of those receiving advisory committee minutes.

While both MCHS programs have MOUs outlining the membership of an advisory group and the responsibilities of partners, each program approached decision making and operational decisions differently. West Kentucky's advisory committee oversees program operation with members sharing in the decision-making process. Since Bluegrass's advisory council was not active at the time this study was conducted, decisions were made by the director in conjunction with the MCHS principal and P–12 district representatives within the college's "academic structure." Even with different structures, partners are involved in the decision-making process and communicated when making decisions.

Several interviewees noted the need for partners to be proactive in creating policies and procedures. One principal stated, "If a student fails a high school class, who is responsible for credit recovery? Are we or the middle college?" A superintendent stated, "I think we started something without policies and procedures. This continues to be a problem. To my knowledge no one is working on these." When asked to provide an example, the superintendent replied, "We need agreements on how sick leave will be paid out and who takes over tenure of faculty."

Both the college presidents and the superintendents indicated that securing funding was critical to sustaining their partnerships. The current grants are coming to an end: If these partnerships, especially Bluegrass, are going to continue operating, finding funding is a must. Because the districts transfer SEEK funding for their participating students, West Kentucky's search for funding is not as urgent. Fourteen of 16 (88%) of survey respondents indicated it was very important to share responsibility in providing and finding funding to operate the MCHS program. Bluegrass's president expressed concerns about not being sufficiently proactive in securing funding, "At this time, I do not know if anyone has a plan to continue when funding is gone. . . . I regret that we did not deal with [this issue] early." A superintendent asserted, "Discussions are needed so that funding is secured to sustain the middle college." Another superintendent expressed, "I do not think the program has become institutionalized and I do not think it will [be] until it is free of grant or foundation funding."

When creating an educational partnership between P–12 and postsecondary education institutions, the presence of a champion was deemed essential by survey respondents. When asked to identify champions of the Bluegrass and West Kentucky programs, it was apparent that champions of these respective programs came from all levels and from both secondary and postsecondary education institutions (e.g., P–12 school district superintendents, college presidents, foundation representatives, and MCHS principals). Interviewed partners shared the skills they believed champions should possess. These skills include, but are not limited to communication skills, building trust, negotiation skills, conflict resolution, and creating a vision. Bluegrass's president maintained the need "to build coalitions." While West Kentucky's president shared, "Demonstrating belief in and sharing information about the partnerships will enable others to become knowledgeable and supportive of these and other educational partnerships."

A final consideration in institutional collaborations is the benefit gained by active engagement in such enterprises. The partner representatives interviewed identified the following benefits for the MCHS collaborative partnerships, presented in order of most often cited at the top:

- Opportunity for students to begin their college education at no cost to them or their parents.
- Attention the college and P–12 school districts have received in various media outlets.
- Increased awareness and importance of secondary partnership among college faculty and staff.
- Students demonstrating an earlier interest in college.
- Improved ACT scores of students involved in program.

Promising Practices

Using interview responses, the following items were identified as promising practices to utilize when creating these types of collaborative partnerships:

- Maintain open and honest communication (all partners).
- Be proactive in creating policies and procedures (all partners).
- Discuss and resolve issues jointly, remaining student focused (all partners).
- Monitor student progress (all partners).
- Develop a process to track students once they leave the program (college presidents and all superintendents).
- Address funding and secure funding early on in the partnership (college presidents and all superintendents).

Implications for Practice

Based on this study, it is recommended that community colleges and P–12 school districts continue to explore avenues that enable them to create institutional partnerships. While there are no concrete guidelines for developing educational partnerships, there are basic elements that can lead to successful creation and maintenance of these types of collaborative efforts. Partners should help all stakeholders understand the partnership and promote the benefits of ongoing collaboration. Until sources of continued funding can be acquired, partners will need to be creative in funding sources to support MCHSs and similar educational initiatives.

If Bluegrass and West Kentucky continue to operate, it will be important to study how their partnerships evolve and mature. Future research should include MCHS faculty, principals, guidance counselors, and parents. The programs will also need to be evaluated and the MCHS graduates followed to determine if program participation made a difference in their futures.

References

Amey, M. J., Eddy, P. L., & Campbell, T. G. (2010, April). Crossing boundaries creating community college partnerships to promote educational transitions. *Community College Review, 37*(4), 333–347.

Amey, M. J., Eddy, P. L., & Ozaki, C. C. (2007). Demands for partnership and collaboration in higher education: A model. In M. J. Amey (Ed.), *New Directions for Community Colleges: No. 139. Collaborations across educational sectors* (pp. 5–14). San Francisco, CA: Jossey-Bass.

Beebe, J. (2001). *Rapid Assessment Process: An introduction.* New York, NY: AltaMira Press.

Blankenship, P., Bolt, W., Mayo, T., & Stephenson, L. (2012). *Technical report on initial two middle college high schools* (Doctoral dissertation). University of Kentucky, Lexington, KY.

Bragg, D. D., Kim, E., & Barnett, E. A. (2006). Creating access and success: Academic pathways reaching underserved students. In D. D. Bragg & E. A. Barnett (Eds.), *New Directions for Community Colleges: No. 135. Academic pathways to and from the community college* (pp. 5–19). San Francisco, CA: Jossey-Bass.

Creswell, J. W. (2009). *Research design: Qualitative, quantitative, and mixed methods approaches* (3rd ed.). Thousand Oaks, CA: Sage.

Cunningham, C. L., & Wagonlander, C. S. (2000). Establishing and sustaining a middle college high school. In J. C. Palmer (Ed.), *New Directions for Community Colleges: No. 111. How community colleges can create productive collaborations with local schools* (pp. 41–51). San Francisco, CA: Jossey-Bass.

Mattessich, P. W., Murray-Close, M., & Monsey, B. R. (2001). *Collaboration: What makes it work* (2nd ed.). St. Paul, MN: Wilder Foundation.

Sink, D. W., Jr., & Jackson, K. L. (2002). Successful community campus-based partnerships. *Community Journal of Research and Practice, 26*(1), 35–46.

LISA G. STEPHENSON *serves as director of West Kentucky Community and Technical College's Community Scholarship Program. She has also provided leadership for the Kentucky Community and Technical College System's Dual Credit Project, overseeing dual credit efforts of the 16 colleges in this system.*

NEW DIRECTIONS FOR COMMUNITY COLLEGES • DOI: 10.1002/cc

2

This chapter introduces effective strategies and practices for working with secondary and postsecondary schools to advance rural Latinas into engineering and other STEM-related fields.

The Role of Secondary School and Community College Collaborations to Increase Latinas in Engineering in a Rural Community

Soko S. Starobin, Glennda M. Bivens

Introduction

The number of high school graduates from rural communities who attend postsecondary institutions is alarmingly low. According to the National Center for Education Statistics (2010), public high schools in rural communities graduate 86.4% of their students compared to students who attend school in cities (71.6%), suburbs (80.8%), and towns (80.2%). Although rural communities are graduating a higher percentage of students from high school compared with other geographical areas in the country, college access among those high school graduates is a problem. While more than 30% of urban adults aged between 25 and older had obtained a college degree in 2000, only 17% of rural adults obtained a college degree (Alliance for Excellent Education, 2010). It is therefore imperative for researchers, school leaders, and communities to understand why students from rural communities graduate at a higher percentage than their geographical counterparts, but attend postsecondary institutions at much lower rates. Research suggests that the lack of high school graduates who attend college from rural communities may be attributed to socioeconomic and personal factors, including career goals and parental educational background (McDonough, Gildersleeve, & Jarsky, 2010). Rural communities often lack physical access to higher education institutions. However, when we look at higher education institutions in rural communities by sector, rural community college campuses represent nearly 60% of all community colleges in the country (Hardy & Katsinas, 2007). These "forgotten majority" institutions of higher

New Directions for Community Colleges, no. 165, Spring 2014 © 2014 Wiley Periodicals, Inc.
Published online in Wiley Online Library (wileyonlinelibrary.com) • DOI: 10.1002/cc.20087

education in rural communities (Starobin & Blumenfeld, 2012) provide educational opportunities for students by leveraging their unique geographical and community characteristics.

The National Science Foundation reports that more than half of all recipients of baccalaureate degrees in science and engineering attended a community college at some point during their academic career (Mooney & Foley, 2011). This is particularly true for Alaskan Native, African American, Asian/Pacific Islander, Latina/Latino, or Native American students. In fact, approximately 51% of Latina and Latino students reported attending a community college prior to earning their bachelor's or master's degrees in science and engineering (Tsapogas, 2004).

In the field of engineering, the number of women who received a baccalaureate increased from 11,135 in 2001 to 12,766 in 2010. Yet the proportion of women as degree recipients in engineering did not mirror the growth of degree recipients. Women accounted for 20.1% of recipients of bachelor's degrees in engineering in 2001, declining to 18.4% in 2010. However, between 2001 and 2010, the number of women who received baccalaureate degrees grew by 14.6% overall. Among underrepresented minority student groups during the same period, Latinas showed the highest growth rate, with 39.9% (from 962 to 1,346), whereas Blacks showed a decrease of 21.7% (from 1,028 to 805). Asian/Pacific Islanders also showed increase (13.9%; from 1,684 to 1,918), but not as high as that of Latinas. From these national statistics, it is timely and relevant to understand how and what contributes to Latina students' decision to pursue an engineering degree. Understanding this student population is critical because there is a growing Latino/a population in many rural communities across the country and because female participation in science, technology, engineering, and mathematics (STEM) fields in higher education does not represent the female population in the United States (National Science Foundation, National Center for Science and Engineering Statistics, 2013).

National student enrollment trends have shown that community colleges serve as an entry point for many Latina high school students who want to attend institutions of higher education. Community colleges offer these students the opportunity to attend schools near their families and within communities familiar to them (Starobin & Laanan, 2010).

This chapter presents findings from a case study that illustrates how a Latina school counselor, with support from Project Lead the Way (PLTW), a national education organization, generated interest among rural Latinas to pursue academic programs in engineering through collaboration with various secondary schools and colleges. It describes how partnerships with a rural middle school and a high school increased the enrollment and retention of Latinas in a pre-engineering program. It also underscores the importance of local professional networks and how they fuel Latina student interest in STEM. The information included in this chapter is designed to help community college administrators and practitioners gain a better understanding of the factors that may contribute to increasing the number of Latina students enrolled in pre-engineering programs.

Paving the Way for Latina Students to Participate in STEM Activities

The students involved in this program attended a rural high school in the Midwest. They were participants of PLTW, a nationally recognized program designed to provide a seamless path for students to college and careers in STEM-related fields for middle school and high school students. Its curriculum focuses on the integration of the applications of science, technology, engineering, and mathematics to hands-on problem solving in STEM fields, especially in engineering and biomedical fields. A high school counselor recruited groups of students for this project through strategic support services and programs to cultivate their interest to participate. She sent students invitations to participate and information about how they can use this pipeline program to reach their educational aspirations, that is, to pursue postsecondary education in engineering by attending a nearby community college and later a university. She also searched and invited important constituents to sustain students' commitment to the program. She solicited support from colleagues from other institutions, and families and citizens in the community, to build a supportive educational environment for these students.

The key organizational partners included a middle school, a high school, a community college, and a public four-year university. Students who graduate from the middle school later attend the high school. Both schools are physically connected by a hallway. The community college offers these high school students the opportunity to take courses on its campus, and students can later transfer to the university to complete a bachelor's degree. The community college has a strong articulation agreement with the college of engineering at the university.

Using Physical Space to Build Educational Partnerships

The counselor supported these students by using physical space within the schools and between the buildings as a tool for establishing close relationships with staff and students. As Willis (2009/2010) suggests, physical space often symbolizes differences between communities. To break any barriers resulting from student perceptions of difference, the counselor leveraged the close proximity between the schools as a way to encourage students to reach for higher academic achievement. The middle school and high school buildings were physically connected in an L-shaped structure, which was used to give students the impression that they attended school in a connected, relationship-oriented environment. While in high school, they took college courses in a nearby building, located on the community college campus. This was particularly useful to the counselor, whose aim was to maintain her visibility between these three schools, as a way to support her efforts to recruit high school students to take college courses. Transportation was provided for students to take classes at the college. This also encouraged student participation.

The Counselor as a Change Agent

The counselor was the primary facilitator of these activities. As a female and a Latina, she spent considerable time developing close relationships with students, school staff, and administrators. In turn, the students felt understood by and connected to her. She spoke fluent Spanish, which she effectively used to connect with the students, and she was familiar with the students' cultural backgrounds. She understood the important roles of their families and others in the rural community where they lived. She held a master's degree and spoke with students about her own experience as a Latina who successfully navigated higher education institutions to earn her credentials. The students did not perceive her as a program recruiter. Rather, they saw her as a familiar, trusted person who attended college, and who invites families of students to join larger families of students. She encouraged them to study STEM fields at the community college and later transfer to the university. She invited Latina students enrolled in a nearby university engineering program to speak with her high school students, to make educational opportunities for them seem realistic. The university students' presentations helped the high school students develop confidence to succeed in PLTW, which also helped to formulate their identities as female students who will study pre-engineering and pursue postsecondary education in STEM fields. The counselor planned high school visits by Latina university students as a strategic measure for helping students become more self-aware and recognize their academic and professional abilities and potential. This helped them feel supported, which enhanced their commitment to succeeding.

It Takes a Village to Support Latina Students

There is a significant increase in the Latino population in the town where these educational institutions are located. Retaining students in this program required a family-centered approach. The counselor interacted with parents in Spanish. She was also effective at facilitating communication between the teachers and administrators who spoke English and those Spanish-speaking parents. The counselor knew from her personal and professional experiences that interacting in one language with those involved is not appropriate for successful student recruitment and retention efforts.

NEW DIRECTIONS FOR COMMUNITY COLLEGES • DOI: 10.1002/cc

We have a presentation in English and then we have one in Spanish. I do the Spanish one. Especially with parents, all the parents want their children to succeed, especially with our population we are about 40 percent Spanish-speaking ... When students sign-up for PLTW, the parents sign the form [permitting a student's participation]. If a student wanted to drop a class, I had to talk to the parent first ... so that the parents know and understand that the students drop the course.

Summary and Conclusion

Effective recruitment and retention of rural Latina students in a pre-engineering program requires unique strategies and practice. Collaboration with counselors from middle and high schools is crucial, as is finding ways to effectively use physical space to develop educational pipelines. A strong leader whose background is similar to the students' and who is knowledgeable about their culture and language is pivotal to advancing students, encouraging parents, and garnering support from English-speaking colleagues.

The authors provide recommendations for policy and practice as well as new directions for community college administrators and practitioners to develop institutional goals and strategies to expand underrepresented student enrollments in STEM fields. When students are from an underrepresented cultural background, teachers, administrators, and staff members should be open to take new directions in their traditional practices and cultural norms that create strong intercampus collaborations. It may be that through a partnership between community college administrators and practitioners, institutions examine how such collaboration offers positive learning opportunities, environment, and physical spaces for students to pursue postsecondary education in STEM fields.

Practitioners Must Understand the Culture of a Community.   Educators who want to advance representation among underrepresented minority students, especially Latinas, must understand and respect the culture of the students and their families. It may be that they value the advancement of a collective, rather than individual achievement. Often, the collective culture pulls away Latina students to advance their education by being away from their family and community. For these reasons, students must be able to connect to faculty and staff who assist them. Practitioners must understand and be constantly aware of the diverse cultural backgrounds of the students they serve, to be perceived by students as trustworthy. This will send a positive message to students and make them more willing to participate in a program designed to support them.

Be Aware of How Students May Perceive Physical Space Within Educational Communities.   Proximity of middle and high schools, community colleges, and universities can impact student perceptions of challenges to earning college degrees. Demystifying the sometimes intimidating and unknown aspects of higher level institutions can often be broken down by a caring, trusted change agent with whom students have developed a positive relationship.

Family and Community Support Are Critical to Encouraging Students to Attend College. It often takes a family and a community network to support Latina students and to encourage them to study at postsecondary institutions in engineering. Support from family and other important individuals can lead to successful recruitment of Latina students.

Show Latina Students That Attending Community College Can Lead to Lifelong Educational Opportunities. Further, community colleges provide lifelong educational opportunities for their communities through adult basic education, noncredit recreational courses, dual-credit courses for high school students, and workforce training opportunities for adults, to name a few. For these reasons, the authors argue that community colleges possess the highest educational and social capital in their respective communities and have the leverage and potential to lead the initiatives to recruit families of traditionally underrepresented populations to pursue higher education.

References

Alliance for Excellent Education. (2010, February). *Current challenges and opportunities in preparing rural high school students for success in college and careers: What federal policymakers need to know.* Washington, DC: Author.

Hardy, D. E., & Katsinas, S. G. (2007). Classifying community colleges: How rural community colleges fit. In P. L. Eddy & J. P. Murray (Eds.), *New Directions for Community Colleges: No. 137. Rural community colleges: Teaching, learning, and leading in the heartland* (pp. 69–78). San Francisco, CA: Jossey-Bass.

McDonough, P., Gildersleeve, R. E., & Jarsky, K. M. (2010). The golden cage of rural college access: How higher education can respond to the rural life. In K. A. Schafft & A. Y. Jackson (Eds.), *Rural education in the twenty-first century: Identity, place, and community in a globalizing world* (pp. 191–209). University Park: The Pennsylvania State University Press.

Mooney, G. M., & Foley, D. J. (2011, July). *Community colleges: Playing an important role in the education of science, engineering, and health graduates* (Info Brief NSF 11-317). Arlington, VA: National Science Foundation. Retrieved from http://www.nsf.gov/statistics/infbrief/nsf11317/nsf11317.pdf

National Center for Education Statistics. (2010). *Digest of Education Statistics 2010, Table 210.* Washington, DC: Institute of Education Sciences, U.S. Department of Education. Retrieved from http://nces.ed.gov/programs/digest/d10/tables/dt10_210.asp

National Science Foundation, National Center for Science and Engineering Statistics. (2013). *Women, minorities, and persons with disabilities in science and engineering: 2013* (Special Report NSF 13-304). Arlington, VA: Author.

Starobin, S. S., & Blumenfeld, W. J. (2012). A model of social ecology of bullying in community colleges: Examining institutional identity based on curricular functions and Carnegie classifications. In J. Lester (Ed.), *Workplace bullying in higher education* (pp. 74–86). New York, NY: Routledge.

Starobin, S. S., & Laanan, F. S. (2010). From community college to Ph.D.: Educational pathways in science, technology, engineering, and mathematics. *Journal of Women and Minorities in Science and Engineering, 16*(1), 71–88.

Tsapogas, J. (2004). *The role of community colleges in the education of recent science and engineering graduates* (Info Brief NSF 4-315). Washington, DC: NSF. Retrieved from http://www.nsf.gov/statistics/infbrief/nsf04315/nsf04315.pdf

Willis, J. (2009/2010). Feminist scholarship and the interrogation of spatial formation: Mapping as a tool for exploring gender and nation. *Transformations: The Journal of Inclusive Scholarship and Pedagogy, 20*(2), 138–153.

SOKO S. STAROBIN is an assistant professor in the School of Education and director of the Office of Community College Research and Policy at Iowa State University.

GLENNDA M. BIVENS is a doctoral student in the School of Education at Iowa State University.

NEW DIRECTIONS FOR COMMUNITY COLLEGES • DOI: 10.1002/cc

3

This chapter explores a grant-sponsored program and examines the role of departmental and institutional collaborations in advancing student performance outcomes. It provides a theoretical framework and a description of best practices for ensuring the success of first-generation urban community college students.

Improving Student Performance Outcomes and Graduation Rates Through Institutional Partnerships

Michael J. Roggow

Establishing academic and student service programs at an institution of higher learning requires buy-in and collaboration on the part of faculty and staff. Such collaborations are essential even at the earliest stages of designing such programs.

In 2009, faculty and staff at Bronx Community College (BCC) and John Jay College of Criminal Justice (JJC), both part of the City University of New York (CUNY) system, came together to write a grant proposal with the dual aim of establishing a program in the growing field of criminal justice and providing a much-needed boost to Hispanic students. The proposal was successful, with the U.S. Department of Education awarding the institutions a $3.7 million grant whose central purpose is helping students graduate with associate and baccalaureate degrees from BCC and JJC, respectively. The grant also aims to support Hispanic high school students in the Bronx, many of whom are first-generation English speakers, as they work to earn an associate's degree in criminal justice at BCC and then transition to JJC to complete their four-year studies.

In 2010, after discontinuing its associate degree programs, JJC began admitting students only into baccalaureate degree programs. Earlier, the College established a new admissions policy, stating that New York City high school graduates who do not meet the academic requirements will be granted admission to the community colleges of the City University of New York (CUNY) and will be admitted to JJC after the completion of an associate's degree. Once the policy was implemented, hundreds of

NEW DIRECTIONS FOR COMMUNITY COLLEGES, no. 165, Spring 2014 © 2014 Wiley Periodicals, Inc.
Published online in Wiley Online Library (wileyonlinelibrary.com) • DOI: 10.1002/cc.20088

high school graduates enrolled in the Criminal Justice Program at BCC. A good number of the students were at-risk for failing, however, because of their level of preparedness in mathematics and writing and because they were first-generation college students for whom English is a second language.

At the time, BCC lacked the necessary resources to accommodate the large influx of students into the Criminal Justice Program and to provide supplementary instruction to help them successfully complete mathematics and writing course requirements. BCC and JJC came together to appeal to the U.S. Department of Education (ED) in order to secure funding to support these students and help them succeed in developmental courses in mathematics and writing, with the ultimate aim of helping them earn an associate's degree and transfer with junior status to JJC.

In 2009, faculty and staff from various academic departments at BCC and JJC worked together to design and secure the $3.7 million ED grant. Provisions from the grant created opportunities for many faculty members from across many disciplines to learn about and eventually put into practice teaching methods geared to improved classroom instruction. It also improved academic and transfer advisement for students, thereby increasing student graduation and transfer rates.

This chapter tells the story of how BCC and JJC planned to write a grant proposal to support student success, and the design of its blueprints. We will discuss how this grant, once it was funded, enabled us to subsidize activities that led to improved student retention, graduation, and retention rates. Finally, we highlight lessons learned and recommendations for best practices.

Designing the Grant Proposal: Planning for Collaborations

A successful grant proposal should, and typically does, reflect the ideas of a wide variety of campus leaders who are committed to addressing institutional challenges. Grant proposals should paint a portrait of institutional partnerships that are interdependent and that show evidence of institutional commitment to improving teaching, advisement, and other activities that promote student success. The U.S. Department of Education's Hispanic-Serving Institution (Title V) five-year grant was awarded to BCC and JJC in 2010 because of its design to support Hispanic students. Its byproduct was to increase student retention and graduation rates. At the heart of this grant, however, is the development of innovative classroom pedagogy and student engagement as well as student advisement. Departmental, divisional, and intrainstitutional collaborations fuel these engines, and this chapter illustrates these designs and some best practices that emerged in teaching and student services.

Student retention and degree completion rates are often viewed as measures of institutional success (Burke & Minnassians, 2003).

NEW DIRECTIONS FOR COMMUNITY COLLEGES • DOI: 10.1002/cc

Graduation rates were among the first three indicators on the original list of *Core Indicators of Effectiveness for Community Colleges* (Alfred, Ewell, Hudgins, & McClenney, 1999). The goals of this grant are to increase both the number of BCC graduates and how many of these graduates transfer to earn their bachelor's degree at JJC. To meet these goals, faculty had to develop new and innovative teaching methods to promote student learning in their classroom. Program administrators had to improve student advisement and supplementary instruction for at-risk BCC students. BCC and JJC faculty and staff collaborate to design clear pathways for students to transfer after they earned their associate's degree. As improving student support resources contributes to higher degree attainment (Ewell, 2011), both institutions had to subsidize tutoring, internships, and support for ESL students. The presidents and provosts of both BCC and JJC wholeheartedly supported this grant proposal, which aims to improve Hispanic student retention and graduation rates as well as college learning resources.

Partnering With High Schools. BCC launched the Criminal Justice Program (CRJ) in 2008 with fewer than 100 enrolled students. Our original strategy then was to increase program enrollment by partnering with and providing academic support for at-risk students at nearby public high schools. Many urban high school students are particularly underprepared for college-level work, especially in mathematics and writing. Consistent with research by Rodriguez, Hughes, and Belfield (2012), dual enrollment programs, which enable high school students to take college courses while they are still in high school, encourage connections between high school and community college career-technical programs. Students often benefit. Dual enrollment programs provide environments in which students "try on" the role of a college student (Karp, 2006), and may be more likely to attend college after they earn a high school diploma.

We also believed a dual enrollment approach might yield increased enrollment for our program. We used grant funds to provide supplemental instruction in these subjects to help students become ready to take college-level courses. BCC targeted its efforts at high school students who planned to declare a major in criminal justice and wanted to eventually earn a bachelor's degree at JJC. Our original plan was to provide tutoring, writing and mathematics workshops, and peer mentoring for these students to increase their likelihood of earning a high school diploma. These academic support tools were also designed to help students pass BCC's entrance exams while they were still in high school. The college would then offer them admission, exempt them from having to complete remedial courses, and then help them create a plan to graduate with an associate's degree in four semesters.

BCC had to modify this plan soon after its inception because program enrollment exceeded institutional capacity within three years. The program decided to invest grant resources to support newly admitted freshmen, most of whom were asked to take remedial courses in mathematics and writing after taking the college placement exam. Some students placed in low-level remedial courses, so program administrators offered free remedial courses for new BCC students. Students took these courses in the summer before the fall term. Those who completed their course and scored high enough to exit remediation were permitted to take college-level courses in the fall. This increases students' likelihood to graduate from BCC earlier than if they would if they started taking remedial courses in their first term. Faculty who teach these summer courses are full- or part-time, and most are chosen to teach these courses because they work effectively with new students and because of their reputation for effectively engaging students in the classroom. Our work with high schools and with new students requires constant collaboration with several academic departments, who assist by identifying and hiring faculty for our program.

Collaborative Efforts With Academic Departments

The Principal Investigator (PI) for this grant is a member of the Office of Academic Affairs management team. The Criminal Justice Program, the key recipient of this grant, is part of the Department of Social Sciences. For this reason, it is crucial that the PI and the department chairperson of Social Sciences work in tandem to offer and promote student tutoring, advising, and cocurricular activities. In time, however, we realized that most students did not struggle with course requirements in the social sciences as much as they did in mathematics and writing. Research by Fong et al. (2013) suggests that mathematics courses are often barriers to success of college students and, in fact, addressing students' developmental needs in mathematics proved to be one of the biggest challenges to this program. Many students need skill development in writing, which poses additional challenges for our program. Program managers work with department chairpersons from English, mathematics, and history to improve students' writing, mathematics, and critical thinking skills. These partnerships are pivotal to helping students complete their remedial-level courses and take college-level mathematics and English courses sooner.

Our students marvel at television shows like "CSI" and "Criminal Minds," sometimes inspiring them to declare a major in criminal justice. When they arrive at BCC, they often want to take courses in the Criminal Justice Program immediately because they want to feel connected to their program of study. Research indicates that student learning is often accelerated when students are motivated to have a reason to learn, and they often learn more when they talk and interact in class about the subject matter. We helped set the stage for them by encouraging faculty to use innovative teaching techniques to deliver course material. They designed special class sections for CRJ students in mathematics, English, and history. Faculty infused applications pertaining to law and justice into their classes to help students become more interested and engaged.

One English professor who teaches a course in literary analysis assigned Jennifer Wynn's (2001) book *Inside Rikers: Stories for the World's Largest Penal Colony.* An observer of this class wrote that "the students were so engaged with the reading on Rikers Island; they were alive, inquisitive, curious, articulate, and spontaneous." Another instructor held a writing contest for CRJ students, in which they were able to write about topics including cyberbullying, digital piracy, privacy, and government surveillance. A mathematics professor engages students by assigning homework requiring them to make calculations and find averages about topics including bank robberies and car chases. We assigned tutors in classrooms to assist instructors. Tutors and instructors strategize to reinforce student learning through small group work, mandatory tutoring, and review sessions outside of class. In-class tutors act as liaisons between students and classroom instructors. Many students find it easier to receive assistance from a peer as opposed to an instructor, and the tutor often knows how to better assist students because he or she is familiar with topics taught in the classroom. One discovery we have made is that in-class tutors are a better investment because they work with students outside the classroom as well. Tutors who work with students on a one-on-one basis during regularly scheduled office hours are often underutilized because students in many cases do not seek their assistance. Also, it is better-prepared students who tend to ask to work with individual tutors, whereas in-class tutors work with students at all levels.

As many college students benefit from Freshman Seminars, many CRJ students register for a special class section of Freshman Seminar (FYS 11). Offered in conjunction with various academic departments, FYS 11 is a single-credit course that integrates academic content with study skills, time management, and career advisement. In addition, students learn about self-awareness and a range of other skills and behaviors needed for success in college-level coursework (Rodriguez et al., 2012). Many BCC students who take this course demonstrate higher course completion rates in their first semester and are more likely to complete their first year of college compared to students who did not take the course. CRJ students who took this course in fall 2012 and spring 2013 completed their first year of college at higher rates. We offered special sections of this seminar for students in our program to keep them together as cohorts and to help them apply their learning to their major, making it easier for academic advisers to monitor their academic progress, thereby reducing attrition. We assigned themes to these special sections to attract student interest. They include Unlocking the Criminal Mind, Searching for Justice, and Bad Guys Have All the Fun. Criminal justice themes are integrated into each of these classes. The CRJ program partners with several legal professionals in New York City who periodically come to campus to speak with students in CRJ classes. They include human rights and immigration lawyers, forensic social workers, former prison inmates, authors, and litigators.

Partnerships That Advance General Education and Assessment

BCC and JJC recognize the importance of designing general-education-based student learning outcomes for their courses and conducting ongoing course assessment to strengthen student learning and performance outcomes. BCC did this by training faculty who teach special sections of English, mathematics, and Freshman Seminar to design embedded learning outcomes to address the learning for CRJ students. These faculty members learned to evaluate student learning using rubrics, scoring tools that lay out specific expectations for a class assignment (Stevens & Levi, 2013). Ewell (2011) suggests embedding assessments in assignments that students must complete in their classes. Maki (2013) indicates that the best learning is supported by helping students apply their learning by helping them make connections to subject matter. To support them, we designed a faculty development program to teach faculty best practices for conducting course assessment and to use these methods to analyze their students' progress and modify their courses along the way and as needed. Course and program assessment are unfamiliar and uncomfortable for many faculty who have never done them and because they are often viewed as time consuming (Ewell, 2011). The BCC Assessment Manager was pivotal to us as we navigated the way to help our program become assessment centered. The Institute for General Education and Assessment, held annually by the American Association for Colleges and Universities (AAC&U), taught us how to initiate a climate of doing assessment, from which we modeled our faculty development activities.

Academic and Student Affairs Partner to Advance Students

Since students are presumed to drop out of college often due to lack of involvement or engagement in the college community (Tinto, 2004) or because they often do not feel sufficiently supported or validated (Barnett, 2006), two CRJ activity coordinators have been enlisted to provide academic advisement and interventions for CRJ students. These advisers work for the Academic Affairs division and are assigned to work exclusively with CRJ students, developing close relationships with these students and carefully monitoring and tracking their academic performance. They also organize cocurricular activities and invite speakers to campus to share their own stories and experiences. Among these speakers are police officers, lawyers, and writers. As CRJ program enrollment grew by an average of 250 students every year from 2010 to 2013, it became clear that there were not enough advisers to accommodate the growing numbers of students. To address this problem, the Office of Academic Affairs began to work together with advisers from the Student Affairs division to ensure our students receive sufficient academic and social support. Advisers from Student Affairs assisted the CRJ program by providing initial advisement and orientation for new

NEW DIRECTIONS FOR COMMUNITY COLLEGES • DOI: 10.1002/cc

students. Many CRJ students have utilized services in the Offices of Psychological Services and Disability Services and have attended lectures and other activities sponsored by Student Affairs. While often those divisions do not communicate well (Philpott, 2003), this partnership was effective and productive, particularly for Spanish-speaking students who request bilingual counselors, many of which work in Student Affairs.

Collaborations With the Office of Institutional Research

Community colleges increasingly face pressure to appropriately use data in their decision-making processes (Hagedorn & Kress, 2008). Institutional researchers control data needed to build effective programs, therefore establishing an effective relationship with IR staff is essential to success (Lillibridge, 2008). The PI's relationship with the BCC Office of Institutional Research is among the most critical. This office enables CRJ program administrators to keep a pulse on information about CRJ student demographics, their rates of retention and academic performance in various subject areas, and numbers of students who complete their associate degrees annually. Close monitoring of student data generated by this office is critical to maintaining or changing course of this program and toward achieving the goals of this grant.

The main objectives proposed for evaluation were to document, interpret, and assess student, faculty, and student learning outcomes, and to make decisions about how to improve our program at midpoints. Our evaluation design included formal assessment, which included formative and summative evaluation. Consistent with recommendations made by Johnston (2011), the BCC Office of Institutional Research assists the CRJ program by helping define student success, interpret negative findings and how to change course, and assess student performance outcomes. An evaluation consultant conducts qualitative evaluation on program activities by interviews, observations, and focus groups.

The Office of Institutional Research assists us by collecting information about student demographics, academic performance, and rate of progress in earning an associate's degree. Our student enrollment fluctuates annually, and the level of college preparation in mathematics and English among newly admitted students changes every year. This office provides information about student course placements, which helps us plan special course sections in English and mathematics. We rely on this information to, for example, make budget decisions regarding remedial courses and tutoring. This information also helps us make decisions about student advisement caseload assignments. The office also helps us identify students who are nearing graduation, so we can conduct outreach to ensure they have met all their course requirements for graduation and to explain the necessary steps for their transfer to JJC.

Institutional Research supports our program by identifying CRJ students who receive poor midterm grades and the courses in which they are underperforming. We use this information to plan interventions and to assist students with creating plans to improve their academic performance. Institutional Research also helps us analyze the effectiveness of our interventions and whether they demonstrate positive impact for struggling students. Institutional Research assists us in designing tools for tracking at-risk students and analyzing academic performance of those who receive tutoring and other support services. This office provides the CRJ program with numbers of students who successfully completed their first year of college, which courses they repeat, success rates of students in required courses compared to all BCC students overall, and the extent to which special classes enhance student success. This office also helps the PI create student satisfaction surveys, which are used for further program planning.

For students who take special classes of FYS 11, the Office of Institutional Research collects and analyzes information about the number of CRJ students enrolled, the number who pass, the semester grade point average for each, and the average number of credits each student completes. This enables us to determine how much progress our students made and whether funding is well spent for this purpose.

Partnering With John Jay College

Many community college graduates become frustrated when their credits do not transfer, as this often results in their incurring more time and expense to earn a bachelor's degree (Mobelini, 2013). Ensuring smooth transfer for BCC graduates is an essential aspect of our partnership with JJC. To facilitate seamless transfer, BCC and JJC appointed a transfer adviser to advise students with 45 of 60 earned credits and register them for junior-level classes at JJC while they are enrolled in their final semester at BCC. These students do not have to apply for admission to JJC; they become automatically matriculated for the following term at JJC as soon as they register for their classes while at BCC. The transfer adviser provides students with individual advisement and invests significant time working with each student. Class space at JJC is reserved for these students to ensure they do not get closed out of important classes in their first term there (R. Bartholomew, personal communication, September 4, 2013). This process has contributed to increased rates of student transfers from BCC to JJC, from 5 students in 2010 to 62 students in 2012.

In addition, we proposed a Summer Bridge Program for student graduates before they enter JJC every term. This was intended to be a cooperative activity developed and implemented by both BCC and JJC faculty. It was also intended to provide BCC graduates with academic seminars designed to better prepare them for advanced coursework in mathematics and criminal justice courses. Our goal was to increase BCC instructor awareness of the linguistic and instructional needs of first-generation Hispanic students by offering workshops and online training modules to increase the number of instructors participating in online training sessions.

Recommendations

The recommendations included here reflect best practices for securing grant funding as well as for administering teaching and student services. Recommendations 1–3 pertain to grant proposals, while 4–6 focus on best practices at an urban community college.

1. Collaborate with and get buy-in from senior administrators, faculty, and staff. Grant writers submit proposals to obtain resources needed to address serious college-wide problems that prevent students from being successful. Administrators and faculty must be fully committed to make critical improvements and eventually institutionalize them. Reviewers often award grants to institutions that show evidence of this. A well-constructed proposal with an organized plan of action and assessment, and one that involves an entire campus, is a good indicator of whether campus leaders are serious about using grant funding effectively.
2. Implement a plan for assessment from the beginning. A plan for assessment should be continuous and key to providing information about whether and how program activities advance student success. It is also integral to strategic planning over the life of the grant and when reviewing or modifying program goals. An Office of Institutional Research should employ a range of assessment methods. Also, an experienced outside evaluation consultant can assess grant activities more closely over an extended time span. A consultant can utilize more advanced assessment tools to evaluate a program and measure progress over time, which will also enable an institution to prepare required annual reports of high quality.
3. Be prepared to reshape grant activities when necessary. Institutional priorities, staffing, course requirements, and student enrollment will change, and that may require college officials to modify grant activities to align them with the goals of the institution. Some initiatives funded by a grant prove ineffective or wasteful, while others yield better student performance outcomes. When an activity proves to be ineffective, or when an alternative activity may more effective, do not be afraid to make changes, as this is to be expected. Grant managers must always keep the funding agency updated about such occurrences.
4. Make tutors available to students in the classroom. Train faculty to work with student tutors to work as partners in delivering classroom

instruction. Student tutors can relate to and assist students in ways that often an instructor cannot, though instructors must work in tandem with the tutor. In-class tutors can assist a broader range of students as opposed to office visits. In-class tutors typically are able to identify students who struggle with courses and are hesitant to ask for assistance. Tutors who are well trained can make other students feel at ease about asking for help. In-class tutoring is also a better use of resources than individual tutoring, especially when student support funding is limited.

5. Promote partnerships between student affairs and institutional research offices. When they work together, these offices can be effective at assessing the progression of students and conducting outreach to those who underperform. Institutional Research often has the capability to query the academic progress of students at semester midpoints and generate lists of students to assist Student Affairs staff in determining which students to invite for advisement and intervention. Each division should share responsibility for tracking the progress of at-risk students and making information about tutoring, library resources, and other resources available to the students. Faculty should provide academic advisers with periodic lists of struggling students, which advisers may then use to conduct intervention activities.

6. Offer faculty development programs and other incentives to instruct faculty on how to infuse major-specific content into courses with high student failure rates. This strategy may cultivate student engagement in a subject matter, which may lead to improved student performance rates. To support this method, faculty should embed and assess course learning outcomes. They should set learning benchmarks for students along the way and continuously analyze student performance. Faculty may be able to improve student learning along the way by changing materials and reevaluating their pedagogical methods.

References

Alfred, R., Ewell, P., Hudgins, J., & McClenney, K. (1999). *Core indicators of effectiveness for community colleges* (2nd ed.). Washington, DC: Community College Press.

Barnett, E. A. (2006). *Validation experiences and persistence among urban community college students* (Master's thesis). Available from ProQuest Dissertations and Theses database. (UMI No. 3250210)

Burke, J. C., & Minnassians, H. (2003). *Performance reporting: "Real" accountability or accountability "Lite"?* Albany: Rockefeller Institute of Government, State University of New York.

Ewell, P. T. (2011). Accountability and institutional effectiveness in the community college. In R. B. Head (Ed.), *New Directions for Community Colleges: No. 153. Institutional effectiveness* (pp. 23–36). San Francisco, CA: Jossey-Bass.

Fong, K., Lebovitz, A., Bashford, J., Harris-Hardland, G., Lebovitz, A., & Bashford, J. (2013, May). *Fast forward: A case study of two community college programs designed to accelerate students through developmental math.* New York, NY: MDRC.

Hagedorn, L. S., & Kress, A. M. (2008). Using transcripts in analysis: Directions and opportunities. In T. H. Bers (Ed.), *New Directions for Community Colleges: No. 143. Student tracking in the community college* (pp. 7–17). San Francisco, CA: Jossey-Bass.

Johnston, G. (2011). The community college IR shop and accreditation: A case study. In R. B. Head (Ed.), *New Directions for Community Colleges: No. 153. Institutional effectiveness* (pp. 53–61). San Francisco, CA: Jossey-Bass.

Karp, M. M. (2006). *Facing the future: Identity development among College Now students* (Doctoral dissertation). Available from ProQuest Dissertation and Theses database. (AAT 3199561)

Lillibridge, F. (2008). Retention tracking using institutional data. In T. H. Bers (Ed.), *New Directions for Community Colleges: No. 143. Student tracking in the community college* (pp. 19–30). San Francisco, CA: Jossey-Bass.

Maki, P. (2013, June). *Taking an inquiry-based approach to designing your assessment.* Lecture conducted from AAC&U Institute for General Education and Assessment, Burlington, VT.

Mobelini, D. C. (2013). Community colleges: Partnerships in higher education. *Community College Journal of Research and Practice, 37,* 629–635.

Philpott, J. L. (2003). On the road to Cambridge: A case study of faculty and student affairs in collaboration. *The Journal of Higher Education, 74,* 77–95.

Rodriguez, O., Hughes, K. L., & Belfield, C. (2012). *Bridging college and careers: Using dual enrollment to enhance career and technical education pathways* (Working Paper). Retrieved from http://www.postsecondaryresearch.org /i/a/document/NCPRWorkingPaper_RodriguezHughesBelfield_DualEnrollment.pdf

Stevens, D. D., & Levi, A. J. (2013). *Introduction to rubrics.* Sterling, VA: Stylus.

Tinto, V. (2004). *Student retention and graduation: Facing the truth, living with the consequences.* Washington, DC: The Pell Institute for the Study of Opportunity in Higher Education.

Wynn, J. (2001). *Inside Rikers: Stories for the world's largest penal colony.* New York, NY: St. Martin's Press.

MICHAEL J. ROGGOW is director of the Criminal Justice Program at City University of New York's Bronx Community College. He is also an adjunct assistant professor of psychology.

4

This chapter explores elements that should be included in a service learning style internship program in urban community colleges. It provides theoretical background and descriptions of best practices for forming community partnerships, collaboratively developing learning outcomes, and aligning program design with institutional general education proficiencies, with a focus on civic learning. Additionally, it illustrates two examples of these measures being implemented and producing their intended effect.

Collaborating for Social Justice Through Service Learning

Tom DePaola

Service learning programs in urban community colleges can be more effective if they focus on social justice issues that impact students and their communities. Through collaborative planning and assessment, this approach can assist in deepening students' critical understanding of their field and honing their civic identities in ways that are individually and collectively meaningful. It is also useful for advancing institutional general education proficiencies.

National Calls to Action Over Civic Learning

In recent years, the imperative to promote civic engagement in higher education has taken a prominent position in the scholarship of general education reform, as evidenced by bold initiatives like Liberal Education and America's Promise (LEAP), which holds civic learning to be an essential outcome that should be basic to every college education (LEAP, 2007). This and other AAC&U publications including *A Crucible Moment: College Learning and Democracy's Future* take very seriously the traditional responsibility of all forms of higher education to produce not merely employable individuals but also active citizens (AAC&U, 2012). AAC&U offers a plethora of resources on civic learning practices that can be useful to any institution seeking to integrate more "high-impact" civic pedagogies including service learning into program offerings (AAC&U, 2014).

New Directions for Community Colleges, no. 165, Spring 2014 © 2014 Wiley Periodicals, Inc.
Published online in Wiley Online Library (wileyonlinelibrary.com) • DOI: 10.1002/cc.20089

37

LEAP notes that civic engagement in higher education is crucial to addressing real, ongoing crises in social justice that threaten to destabilize the vitality of American democracy (LEAP, 2007). *A Crucible Moment*, likewise, stresses that the push to create a robust culture of civic engagement is particularly needed in community colleges, as many of these students come from poor or otherwise marginalized communities to seek a path to upward mobility. At Bronx Community College (BCC), for instance, the vast majority of students come from local communities faced with long histories of pervasive inequality and marginalization. If urban community colleges can devise thoughtful, innovative programming that mobilizes their students around shared civic values and concerns, the cumulative effects over time on the communities they serve could be profound.

Student Marginalization and Service Learning

Service learning is a common strategy for promoting civic engagement in higher education but demands extra care when working with urban community college students. Jay Brandenberger (2013), in his article on personal development outcomes in service learning, asserts a need for "developmental sensitivity" on the part of those involved in coordinating community-based activities. By this, he means that they need to always ask: "What do students bring to the encounters offered? What personal factors will be activated?" (p. 144). To group urban community college students together as "marginalized" is not to homogenize them. Though these students may all share a legacy of oppression, this oppression operates in many different domains. Students may come from poverty; they may be people of color, immigrants, or children of immigrants; they may be disabled; they may identify as LGBTQ in a culture hostile to homosexuality; or they may be single parents, veterans, or nontraditional age learners (Harbour & Ebie, 2011; Hardiman & Jackson, 1997). It is critical that the challenges intrinsic to urban community college students are understood as a *plurality* in which social and economic inequality can assume many overlapping forms. In his canonical essay, *Experience and Education*, John Dewey (1938) describes how students can develop purposes in life through learning experiences that empower them to act into the future. But this process necessarily entails facing the past: "The institutions and customs that exist in the present and that give rise to present social ills and dislocations did not arise overnight. They have a long history behind them" (p. 77). Dewey clearly acknowledges that social inequality does not exist in a vacuum. In order for students to deal with the problems of the present, and thereby build a meaningful future, it is crucial that they grasp the historical structures that spawned them. To break out of a cage one must first see the bars.

The diverse life experiences of these students can produce an inchoate discontent with social inequality that may not be easily mobilized toward uniform democratic ends. This challenge should inform planning for the collaborative design of individualized service learning experiences catered to the unique disposition of each participant. Jameson, Clayton, and Ash (2013) encourage more researchers to study the effects of service learning on the development of *civic identity*, a term for the extent that a person's sense of self reflects an understanding of his or her role in the community and a desire to address issues of public concern. To put it another way, civic identity deals in qualities and values traditionally associated with good citizenship. Jameson et al. maintain that a service learning experience can serve as a trigger of civic identity, helping students to realize their capacity as civic agents. Infusing collaborative and reflective elements into any service learning program can be particularly beneficial for urban community college students, who may have weak civic identities or ambivalent attitudes toward civic engagement to begin with.

Building a Socially Responsible Internship Program

Bronx Community College has begun to lay the groundwork for a collaborative, sustainable, social-justice-oriented internship program for students majoring in criminal justice. There are three salient elements to this program, which are designed to foster civic learning and support other general education proficiencies in urban community college students: (a) the identification of placement sites that encourage students to think critically about social issues impacting their communities as well as their chosen field; (b) collaboration with internship partners to develop learning objectives that account for both organizational/community needs and student interests, attitudes, and abilities; and (c) opportunities for students to reflect on and draw connections between their experiences and in-class learning. The sections that follow elaborate on and illustrate with specific examples these measures, which are designed to acknowledge the effects of marginalization on students' understanding of and access to the tools of democratic participation. The strategy works by building on students' strengths and inclinations to develop their sense of civic identity. Through active collaboration, students can acquire the skills necessary to exercise their latent civic agency in democratically productive ways. Furthermore, at BCC, we have discovered such an approach can also serve the institutional mission and support general education objectives.

Partnering With Sites That Encourage Students to Critically Understand Social Issues Impacting Their Communities As Well As Their Chosen Field. The authors of the LEAP manifesto pointedly suggest that students be provided with more opportunities to examine the social and ethical dimensions of their prospective field. Encouraging students to deploy and negotiate their civic values in the real world while furthering their course of study is developmentally paramount. They argue that regardless of how technical or apolitical a career may seem, every field constitutes a "community of practice" (LEAP, 2007, p. 39). As such, no vocation can be considered objectively value-neutral, because none can be entirely divorced from questions concerning power and equality.

Brandenberger (2013) believes the existing research demonstrates conclusively that service learning influences students' sociopolitical attitudes and civic behaviors. In a study led by Mary Prentice and Gail Robinson (2012) for the Community College National Center on Community Engagement, 76% of students who participated in service learning projects as part of their coursework claimed to have a better understanding of their roles as community members. At the same time, researchers need to continue building on emerging models of research characterized by "rich conceptions of civic learning that include knowledge, skills, and the creation of an action-oriented civic identity" (Battistoni, 2013, p. 119). BCC's internship program utilizes postinternship surveys to generate qualitative assessment data each semester. The feedback helps us to evaluate organizational and community impact, and reinforces the partnership as it moves forward by maintaining a dialogue around shared goals. Analysis of final reports written by student participants allows us to assess whether civic learning outcomes and other college outcomes have been adequately met.

What became apparent as BCC's program progressed was that the most successful arrangements employed a collaborative pedagogy of inquiry-based problem solving, but one which was tempered by a developmental sensitivity to the often difficult life experiences that condition each learner with a unique set of biases. This allows us to proceed organically from whichever level of civic development the student happens to occupy to create individualized experiences that are maximally productive in stimulating civic growth.

Collaborative Development of Learning Outcomes That Account for Both Organizational/Community Needs and Student Background, Interests, Attitudes, and Capacities. Collaboration with partner sites to create learning outcomes tailored to fit the needs and abilities of all parties involved is essential. It is important to remember, however, as Bringle & Clayton (2013) note, that these parties "often have different cultures, interests, perspectives, experiences, resources, roles, and power" that must be considered along the way (p. 542). Creating assignments in conjunction with intern supervisors assists in the creation of a campus–community partnership that is reciprocal, even transformational—that is, capacity-building for all involved (Littlepage & Gazely, 2013). Pedagogically, this strategy can open doors to a variety of general education outcomes, as the examples presented later on will illustrate.

Collaboration is also key to developing students' emerging sense of civic agency. As Barbara Jacoby (2013) mentions in her article on frameworks for service learning partnerships, rendering students into responsible, active citizens "requires a set of skills and knowledge that may be more likely to accrue to students who serve as service learning partners rather than simply participants" (p. 604). When students have a say in their roles during the service learning experience, they may be more likely to feel invested in the projects undertaken and experiences had. Partner sites, in turn, are more likely to genuinely benefit from their participation. This kind of collaborative, transformative partnership, which is grown equitably and sustainably, has institutional benefits as well. Over time, networks of such partnerships can emerge and provide an ongoing supply of venues to support general education through socially just experiential learning.

At BCC, we have discovered that collaborating with students to design projects and outcomes using a strength/interest-based approach strongly encourages personal growth outcomes. At the same time, collaboration with partner sites creates an authentic context for applied, problem-based learning; students can exercise their civic agency in a way that is linked to tangible community and organizational progress.

Intentional Opportunities for Students to Reflect and Synthesize Their Experiences With Academic Knowledge and Skills. Reflection is an absolutely indispensable component to civic growth. Paulo Freire is widely recognized for his contribution to pedagogical theory designed to benefit students from marginalized communities (AAC&U, 2012; Brandenberger, 2013; Jacoby, 2013). In his seminal work *Pedagogy of the Oppressed,* Freire (1970) elaborates on how action and reflection are pedagogically inextricable. His analysis shows that above all, critical thinking and identity formation are best enhanced when action and reflection work as a fundamentally concurrent, recursive process (Jacoby, 2013). Research into cognitive outcomes of service learning by Fitch, Steinke, and Hudson (2013) indicates that "reflection activities can encourage students not only to make meaning of the service learning experience in the context of course content but also to use course content to solve problems they encounter in the community and to examine their own ways of knowing, learning, and self-regulating" (p. 73). Ideally, service learning is an active lesson in civic agency and community empowerment, giving students practice with the tools and processes of collaborative action on behalf of shared values. At the same time, the service learning experience functions as an arena in which students can critically evaluate their own epistemologies and learning through reflection and synthesis.

As part of the CRJ internship program at BCC, each student must keep a journal throughout the experience and submit a final report in which he or she is instructed to respond to the following: (a) what was accomplished by the end of the three-month internship; (b) the challenges faced and how they were overcome; (c) how the experience resonates with knowledge gleaned from the student's academic work; and (d) how the experience may or may not have impacted the student's views on his or her own personal career path. This is entirely consistent with BCC's (2012) statement on general education proficiency, "Personal Growth and Professional Development," which says: "Use continued self-development to examine personal values and civic responsibilities" ("General Education Proficiencies," point 6). Reflective exercises can magnify this objective, augmenting critical gains made during the experience by converting it into concrete expression, which can then be utilized for evaluation purposes.

Research suggests the products of student reflection are crucial for assessment, to be analyzed individually or collectively by faculty for evidence of critical thinking and other qualitative benchmarks of program effectiveness (Clayton, Hess, Jaeger, Jameson, & McGuire, 2013). These, along with data from partner feedback, have been instrumental in expanding and refining the internship program in a sustainable, equitable, and pedagogically sound fashion.

Socially Responsible Service Learning in Action

The sections that follow describe two separate internships that exemplify how development through this kind of service learning can unfold in students with fledgling but unfocused civic identities. At times, direct quotations from interns' reflections are used to illustrate the emergence of critical thinking and other general education objectives as a result of the experience.

Example 1.   Last year, the BCC Criminal Justice Program formed a partnership with a renowned activist law firm. The goal was to provide internship opportunities for criminal justice students where they could explore how progressive legal action can alter the social justice landscape. The firm is lauded for its role in a case that dissolved certain state laws linked to discrimination of LGBTQ people. The case is emblematic of how legal activism can work to redefine what constitutes a criminal under more equitable terms—a solid point of meditation for someone pursuing a degree in criminal justice.

The first intern we placed with this organization had grappled with his fair share of marginalization: a nontraditional age, Latino student from a low-income family who also identified himself as LGBTQ and for whom English was not his first language. While research indicates that nontraditional age students are often good candidates for experiential learning programs because they tend to be more strategic about their reasons for attending college (Largent, 2013), this student knew only that he wanted ultimately to pursue a career in law, but did not know in what capacity. He jumped at the opportunity to intern with the firm, having first become interested in its work during a lecture on campus by one of its staff attorneys.

Conversations between the student, the supervising attorney, and the BCC Internship Coordinator determined learning outcomes that catered to this particular internship. The student was bilingual and expressed interest in assisting with community outreach. The supervising attorney conceived of a project in which the student would perform outreach to LGBTQ advocacy groups and community organizations in Puerto Rico. The dual goal of this project would be to survey the legal landscape for LGBTQ discrimination cases the firm might pursue that would further its activist mission as well as to develop a resource document organizing the network of contacts the student would acquire in the process. The assignment was not only developed collaboratively; it was intrinsically collaborative in that the substance of the project was to form relationships on behalf of the firm. It allowed the student to ground his basic knowledge of the criminal justice system in an activist experience that oriented his educational/vocational trajectory and honed his civic identity around issues meaningful to him. Furthermore, the experience exposed the student to the mechanics of dismantling oppressive structures in a way that rendered the process comprehensible, rather than abstract, as he conveys in his final reflection:

> Returning to school after more than 20 years, I was not certain what route I wanted to proceed academically and professionally. I had been attracted to the idea of becoming a lawyer for some time, but I saw it as a long and arduous road. Working alongside [the firm's] lawyers, I was finally convinced of this calling and now wish to pursue legal social activism. The best part about doing an internship was having an opportunity to interact with real lawyers and see how they operate in the field. As a result, it no longer feels like something abstract and far off but something achievable.

This passage suggests that the student has crossed a personal development threshold where he begins to conceive of his identity in relation to the sociopolitical circumstances that reinforce structural inequality. In turn, he begins to imagine a vocational context that feels ethically and civically authentic. In another instance, the student describes the emotional challenges he faced while executing the assigned project:

> At times, listening to victims and the hate crimes they endured while having nowhere to seek legal counsel was painful. I was heartbroken by the end of many conversations and my eyes filled with tears. But I feel blessed to have had the opportunity to contribute directly to this important cause. I became educated extensively about laws affecting Puerto Rico's LGBT community and the widespread discriminatory attitude toward gays and lesbians displayed openly by the authorities and media there.

Research in the *Community College Journal of Research and Practice* on best practices in service learning for nontraditional age students suggests that a major indicator of civic learning with these students is whether the participants feel like their actions have a real impact on the community (Largent, 2013). Not only does this student feel that he made a meaningful contribution to a cause with which he sympathizes but also the experience appears to have galvanized his determination to pursue a career path of lifelong advocacy.

In addition to the aforementioned outcomes, the internship also provided the student with an exercise in global citizenship, mobilizing his bilingualism toward community service across international borders. This is consistent with BCC's Global Learning Outcomes (Bolt, 2009), which were adopted by the college in 2009 to include "Acquisition of Global Perspectives," "Cross-Cultural Communication," and "Application of Skills in Local and Global Contexts." As a direct result of the collaborative work between the institution, the student, and the organization, BCC was able to develop a unique service learning experience that integrated multiple core proficiencies while encouraging personal and vocational identity formation. Currently, this student is in the final year of his BA in political science and is making preparations to apply to law school.

Example 2.   In another instance, a student was placed with a grassroots political activist and legal advocacy nonprofit organized around social justice issues affecting New York City's Latino communities. This partnership was formed with the goal of providing internship opportunities for students interested in local policy and criminal justice reform.

The student BCC ultimately placed there was 19-years old, read the newspaper, and enjoyed talking about national politics. He had first become aware of the Internship Program at one of our "Internship Day" events, where professionals from the nonprofit and legal sectors speak to criminal justice students about how their internship experiences strategically focused their careers and exposed them to new possibilities. (After students complete the program, they are also invited to speak at these events.) This student said he wanted to pursue an internship in order to learn to write better. He was interested in law but had developed a taste for reading philosophy in his spare time.

The three parties once again negotiated learning objectives for the internship by considering the student's interests and the organization's capacity to productively accommodate them, and then refined them to reflect on BCC general education proficiencies. The student was brought onboard as a Communications and New Media Intern. He was charged with thoroughly researching the New York City Police Department's controversial "stop and frisk" policy—an issue with which he had some familiarity—in order to write an article to be published on the organization's website. Additionally, he reported on protests around the city through social media and provided administrative support to the organization's lawyers working on the stop and frisk issue.

Not only was the student exposed to the nuts and bolts of social and legal activism, but he was also engaged in active, problem-based learning that fostered his research and composition skills. In his article, the student demonstrates his critical thinking of the stop and frisk dilemma:

> What many police officers don't understand is that these encounters create harsh relationships between the police and the residents, making it more difficult to deter crime from lack of communication. The police end up being viewed as bullies, and crime inevitably increases.

These insights suggest that his engagement with the issue goes beyond a superficial treatment. The project he completed left him with a tangible product of his efforts that both demonstrates a sustained application of skills and contributes directly to a social justice movement pertinent to both his major and his identity. The student later reflects on the impact of the experience:

> Working for [this organization] has had a tremendous influence on my long-term goals and career plans. After my internship, I find myself with a strong desire to go to law school to pursue a career in public interest law. I hope only that someday I can say I helped to mold society in a more positive direction.

Overall, the arrangement cultivated BCC's Personal Growth and Professional Development proficiency, which includes language concerning the development of personal values and civic responsibility. It also provided a real-world context for furthering the communications proficiency. Several months after the student completed his internship at BCC, he was able to parlay his experience into a six-month internship with a member of the New York City Council who is active in police reform.

Conclusion

In 1947, the President's Commission on Higher Education boldly contended that *democracy*, over and above economics, should be the animating force of the community college, setting a precedent for the next seven decades and beyond. That is not to say employment was not an important factor—it certainly was, especially as waves of veterans returned to civilian life following World War II. Nevertheless, the Commission firmly asserted that these ought to be local institutions defined by their intimate relations to the life of the communities in which they are ensconced (Pusser & Levin, 2009). The question is: in today's climate, how does the urban community college live up to this ideal? How do the institutions with the fewest resources, educating students with the most challenges, fulfill the founding intention of the community college and produce not merely employable individuals but active citizens as well?

The answer, this chapter suggests, is that insofar as the strategy includes service learning style internships, they should consciously address the interplay of students' fields of study with issues of inequality that impact their own communities. This fosters civic engagement by providing opportunities to explore their career endeavors in conjunction with an emerging ethic of civic responsibility searching for meaningful expression. Not only can this strategy deepen institutional support for civic engagement, but it can also be a more effective vehicle to advance other general education proficiencies when adjusted to the particular dynamics of each arrangement. This requires collaboration across multiple channels, bridging students, institution, and community through partnerships that have the potential to support long-term social transformation.

This chapter provides three interconnected strategies for pursuing this through a service learning internship program: (a) forming partnerships designed to cultivate a critical awareness of social issues that affect the students themselves; (b) collaborating with the student and partner organization to design an experience that benefits both parties, while also advancing institutional proficiencies; and (c) thoroughly integrating both action and reflection into the service learning pedagogy. If urban community colleges genuinely seek to create a civically literate student body with the wherewithal to participate in the democratic process, they will need to continue to find ways of developing students' latent civic identities through innovative, collaborative programming. The analysis presented suggests that part of the responsibility of the urban community college is literally to empower individuals with the tools to resist their own oppression. As a rule, educators at these institutions should recognize the magnitude of that task.

References

Association of American Colleges and Universities (AAC&U). (2012). *A crucible moment: College learning and democracy's future, a national call to action*. Washington, DC: Author. Retrieved from http://www.aacu.org/civic_learning/crucible/documents/crucible_508F.pdf

Association of American Colleges and Universities (AAC&U). (2014). *Civic learning resources*. Retrieved from http://www.aacu.org/resources/civicengagement/index.cfm

Battistoni, R. M. (2013). Civic learning through service learning. In P. Clayton, R. Bringle, & J. Hatcher (Eds.), *Research on service learning* (Vols. 2A–2B, pp. 111–132). Sterling, VA: Stylus.

Bolt, J. (2009). *Bronx Community College global learning outcomes*. Retrieved from http://www.bcc.cuny.edu/nationalcenterforeducationalalliances/?page=Global_learning_Outcomes

Brandenberger, J. W. (2013). Investigating personal development outcomes in service learning. In P. Clayton, R. Bringle, & J. Hatcher (Eds.), *Research on service learning* (Vols. 2A–2B, pp. 133–156). Sterling, VA: Stylus.

Bringle, R., & Clayton, P. H. (2013). Conceptual frameworks for partnerships in service learning. In P. Clayton, R. Bringle, & J. Hatcher (Eds.), *Research on service learning* (Vols. 2A–2B, pp. 539–572). Sterling, VA: Stylus.

Bronx Community College (BCC). (2012). *Objectives and proficiencies.* Retrieved from https://www.bcc.cuny.edu/GeneralEducation/?page=Objectives_and_Proficiencies

Clayton, P. H., Hess, G. R., Jaeger, A. J., Jameson, J. K., & McGuire, L. E. (2013). Theoretical perspectives and research on faculty learning in service learning. In P. Clayton, R. Bringle, & J. Hatcher (Eds.), *Research on service learning* (Vols. 2A–2B, pp. 245–278). Sterling, VA: Stylus.

Dewey, J. (1938). *Experience and education.* New York, NY: Simon & Schuster.

Fitch, P., Steinke, P., & Hudson, T. (2013). Research and theoretical perspectives on cognitive outcomes of service learning. In P. Clayton, R. Bringle, & J. Hatcher (Eds.), *Research on service learning* (Vols. 2A–2B, pp. 57–84). Sterling, VA: Stylus.

Freire, P. (1970). *Pedagogy of the oppressed.* New York, NY: Continuum.

Harbour, C. P., & Ebie, G. (2011). Deweyan democratic learning communities and student marginalization. In E. M. Cox & J. S. Watson (Eds.), *New Directions for Community Colleges: No. 155. Marginalized students* (pp. 5–14). San Francisco, CA: Jossey-Bass.

Hardiman, R., & Jackson, B. W. (1997). Conceptual foundations for social justice courses. In M. Adams, L. A. Bell, & P. Griffin (Eds.), *Teaching for diversity and social justice* (pp. 16–29). New York, NY: Routledge.

Jacoby, B. (2013). Student partnerships in service learning. In P. Clayton, R. Bringle, & J. Hatcher (Eds.), *Research on service learning* (Vols. 2A–2B, pp. 599–618). Sterling, VA: Stylus.

Jameson, J. K., Clayton, P. H., & Ash, S. L. (2013). Conceptualizing, assessing, and investigating academic learning in service learning. In P. Clayton, R. Bringle, & J. Hatcher (Eds.), *Research on service learning* (Vols. 2A–2B, pp. 85–110). Sterling, VA: Stylus.

Largent, L. (2013). Service-learning among nontraditional age community college students. *Community College Journal of Research and Practice, 37,* 296–312.

Liberal Education and America's Promise (LEAP). (2007). *College learning for the new global century: A report from the national leadership council for liberal education & America's promise.* Washington, DC: Association of American Colleges and Universities. Retrieved from http://www.aacu.org/leap/documents/GlobalCentury_final.pdf

Littlepage, L., & Gazely, B. (2013). Examining service learning from the perspective of community organization capacity. In P. Clayton, R. Bringle, & J. Hatcher (Eds.), *Research on service learning* (Vols. 2A–2B, pp. 419–440). Sterling, VA: Stylus.

Prentice, M., & Robinson, G. (2012, May 24). *Assessing service learning outcomes and telling the story.* Community College National Center for Community Engagement Annual Conference, Scottsdale, AZ.

Pusser, B., & Levin, J. (2009). Re-imagining community colleges in the 21st century: A student-centered approach to higher education. *Center for American Progress Special Report,* 1–49. Retrieved from http://www.americanprogress.org/wp-content/uploads/issues/2009/12/pdf/community_colleges_reimagined.pdf

TOM DEPAOLA *is an adjunct instructor and administers the Criminal Justice internship program for the division of Academic Affairs at Bronx Community College (CUNY).*

NEW DIRECTIONS FOR COMMUNITY COLLEGES • DOI: 10.1002/cc

5

This case study describes five phases that a community college went through in developing its use of knowledge management practices to improve their student outcomes and recommends how other colleges can similarly benefit from knowledge management in meeting their goals.

Turning Knowledge Into Success: The Role of Collaboration in Knowledge Management Implementation

Handan Hizmetli

> Just as ecosystems rejuvenate themselves through cycles and seasons, educational organizations grow and revitalize themselves through the knowledge they create, their processes for passing that knowledge on to others, and the exchanges and relationships that they foster among people.
>
> (Petrides & Nodine, 2003, p. 10)

This chapter explores how an urban community college applied knowledge management (KM; Petrides & Nodine, 2003) over a series of projects to successfully improve student performance. The success of the knowledge management processes stemmed from the collaborative manner in which people and technology were brought together. Collaboration between key college offices and departments played a significant role in establishing and broadening a knowledge management culture. Resulting from this process was the complete revamping of the college's first-year program (FYP), including a fully revised first-year seminar course. The impact of the first-year initiative was immediate. Students who took the revised first-year seminar course were 6% more likely to persist the following semester when compared to students who did not.

Like many community colleges, our college had a long history of seeking out and implementing strategies to address its chronic low student retention and graduation rates. Despite numerous isolated assessment activities and intervention programs over the years, student retention and graduation rates have remained low, recently even experiencing declines.

NEW DIRECTIONS FOR COMMUNITY COLLEGES, no. 165, Spring 2014 © 2014 Wiley Periodicals, Inc.
Published online in Wiley Online Library (wileyonlinelibrary.com) • DOI: 10.1002/cc.20090

College-wide action became crucial. Through the leadership of the associate dean for Institutional Research, our college began experimenting with managing available information to create knowledge about improving student outcomes. Encouraged by the potential for KM to better understand and address the college's flagging retention and graduation rates, the dean fostered the practice of knowledge management in successive and collaborative cross-institutional initiatives.

After a brief discussion about the theory underlying KM practice, we will present five distinct phases of collaborative knowledge management practice, which at our college culminated in the development of a new first-year program. Collaboration across units in the college was encouraged via opportunities for problem identification, information sharing, and reflection on what was being learned. Each phase improved and broadened the college's knowledge about where and how to focus its energy to improve student success. Each phase also prepared collaborators to take on even larger roles in subsequent phases (Petrides & Nodine, 2003). As such, this chapter provides a valuable case study for understanding how collaboration and knowledge management are best integrated in educational organizations to accomplish institutional goals.

The Theory of Knowledge Management Practice in Higher Education Institutions

Increased accountability pressures on higher education institutions means that colleges must seek better ways to use information and knowledge to improve institutional decision making and better student performance (Petrides & Nodine, 2003). The theory underlying KM practice revolves around the systematic and organizationally specified acquisition, organization, and communication of knowledge so that employees may make use of it to be more effective and productive managers of change (Sedziuviene & Vveinhardt, 2009). KM involves four basic knowledge processes: (a) creating knowledge through employees' sharing of knowledge across the organization, (b) storing and retrieving that knowledge, (c) transferring knowledge between units and employees, and (d) applying knowledge to organizational change (Alavi & Leidner, 2001). In today's "big data" world, information technologies (ITs) are the primary bridge between all of these processes. Those information technologies designed specifically to facilitate the sharing and integration of knowledge in an organization are referred to as knowledge management systems (KMS; Alavi & Leidner, 1999). These systems are seen as crucial to the success of knowledge management processes and key precursors to creating actionable knowledge indicators.

While much has been written about KM processes and the role of IT in these processes, very little attention has been paid to the role that collaboration plays in KM practice in institutions of higher education. Collaboration among horizontally and vertically aligned colleagues is necessary for the meaningful and relevant application of KM's four processes. Individuals must share a certain knowledge base in organizations to arrive at the same understanding of data and information available to them (Alavi & Leidner, 2001). Only via collaboration are individuals able to share information and create a common knowledge base in colleges. Collaboration facilitates an elaborated and common knowledge base that allows higher education institutions to answer the questions:

- "What is occurring here?"
- "How is this occurring?"
- "How can we affect the change we want?"

Knowledge management concerns itself with a data-information-knowledge continuum (Petrides & Nodine, 2003) since answering these questions necessitates turning raw data into actionable knowledge. In this continuum, Petrides and Nodine (2003) define data as "facts or quantitative measures." Data only become information "when humans place them in context through interpretation" (p. 13). Information becomes knowledge when "people react to and use the information that is available to them" (p. 13). Alavi and Leidner (1999, p. 5) suggest that knowledge is "information made actionable." For our purposes here, we are highlighting the value that knowledge has in changing policies and guiding creation of intervention aimed at improving student outcomes. This iterative cycle through which data are interpreted, shared, and reinterpreted to guide action necessarily involves collaboration as people continually connect back to and focus on outcomes.

Two types of knowledge are widely discussed in the literature under the knowledge management framework: tacit and explicit. Emerging from action in context, tacit knowledge is "know-how." However, tacit knowledge is hard to articulate and transfer between people and units in organizations such as colleges. Explicit knowledge is linked with "know-what" and is relatively easy to articulate and codify. Tacit knowledge provides the necessary context and the background to understand and interpret explicit knowledge (Alavi & Leidner, 2001). In what follows, we will highlight examples of these dimensions of knowledge.

With this theoretical background now we turn to the five phases that the college went through to arrive at a full circuit of the implementation of knowledge management practices with particular attention to the role of collaboration between Institutional Research and Information Technology. The first three phases will outline the process of establishing the data-information-knowledge continuum. The fourth and fifth phases will describe how the college established a student success initiative—the revamped first-year experience—as a result of this knowledge management process.

Phase I: Establishing a Technology Infrastructure to Facilitate Data Organization and Access

The access to data and data systems is a necessary precursor to the establishment of knowledge management (Chu, Wang, & Yuen, 2011). In the development of a long-term vision to empower faculty, students, and staff with information to support institutional and student success (Ruiz & Ritze, 2003), our institutional research and information technology offices began collaborating nearly a decade ago. Their vision was to create a knowledge-empowered community at the college. Staff from these offices mutually identified that the college's information technology infrastructure was not effective in providing ready access to information (i.e., databases) and analytical tools (e.g., report querying). The technology environment comprised old computer data systems and limited resources. Their goal was to provide current, meaningful, and actionable information to the right people at the right time to support effective decision making.

During 2003–2004, staff from these two offices developed a "mirror" (in Microsoft Access) of the college's antiquated relational student information system. Following the mirror's creation, virtually real-time information became available through information technology applications for administrative and operational decision support and institutional research analyses. It also helped IT take the next step in supporting knowledge management by creating a web portal that included one-stop-shopping e-services. This web portal provided multiple communication channels in the college by bringing information together from faculty and students (online registration, e-attendance and e-grading applications, e-alerts, and e-messages).

Phase II: Converting Data Into Information

The second phase involves the transformation of raw data into information. A university-wide student success initiative, which came shortly on the heels of developing the student database mirror, spurred this conversion. The staff who worked on this initiative realized that the college had yet to develop a clear consensus about the meaning of the data and some administrative information (e.g., class rosters) that had recently become available to them. Staff assigned to this initiative agreed that creating a consensus about student progress and success would empower users of the information. Before that, however, data had to be converted into information. The author initiated a longitudinal regression analysis to answer two major questions to serve this effort: What role do student demographic and academic characteristics play in their retention and graduation? And, how does academic performance in students' first year affect their retention and graduation?

The study found that net of student characteristics, academic progress, and the likelihood of graduation were highly associated with key milestones in the first two semesters (Hizmetli & Ritze, 2010). These milestones were satisfying skill-need requirements (mathematics, reading, and writing) and course performance (i.e., grades). Student background characteristics were not as highly correlated with success except for GED status. GED recipients were less likely to persist to their second semester. OIR followed this study with more specific analyses to deepen the college's understanding of these findings. These analyses identified that indicators generated even earlier— among them, attendance during the first weeks and midterm grades—were an important determinant of end-of-term grades. At this juncture, the college was developing a better sense of the data related to student progress and improvement, and what sorts of analyses could be conducted to create information.

Phase III: Creating a Common Knowledge Base About Student Success

The IR analyses and findings described above fall into the category of explicit knowledge (Chu et al., 2011). These were shared with the college community along with selected literature about student progress and success at various venues and meetings. Engagement of the campus community in discussion of these findings (i.e., explicit knowledge) was crucial so that faculty, staff, and administrators could contribute their experiential (i.e., tacit) knowledge. The discourse between the explicit and tacit knowledge frontiers helped create a common and embedded knowledge base about student success with a particular emphasis on actionable indicators. One feature of this process was the incorporation of overlooked indicators of student progress such as midterm grades, progress grades, attendance, first-semester academic standing, and skill status. However, midterm grades became available too late in the student information system to be of use to faculty, advisers, or counselors. To compensate for this, collaborators created a new actionable "progress grade" to be collected from faculty by the end of the third week of the semester. The thought was that this progress grade would be as effective as the midterm grade in establishing an early alert trigger, but would be available earlier. Some of the factors that faculty were asked to consider in assigning progress grades included student participation in class discussions, assignment completion, and attendance. Progress grades consisted of one of the three choices: exceeds expectations, meets expectations, and does not meet expectations.

Phase IV: Integrating Knowledge Base Indicators in Information Systems

Identification and deployment of the actionable knowledge indicators in Phase III was pivotal for IT's development of digital tools and communication systems to provide real-time and actionable information to students and advisers. As Alavi and Leidner (1999) pointed out, KM practice needs to take advantage of "modern information technologies (e.g., the Internet, intranets, browsers, data warehouses, and software agents) to systematize, facilitate, and expedite firm-wide knowledge management" (p. 2). This took place in two steps at our college (Ruiz & Ritze, 2009). First, IT developed an academic advisement case management system that involved the assignment of every student at the college to a faculty or counseling adviser. This system provided advisers with electronic rosters that refreshed throughout the semester with real-time attendance and performance information for all students in each advisement caseload. Second, IT developed an e-contact management system, whereby students were contacted systematically regarding critical events in the pursuit of an associate's degree. This system was set up by IT to collect data from various sources to alert students, faculty, and advisers to at-risk student behaviors while time still exists to take corrective action.

To assess the effectiveness of incorporating a case management system on retention, collaborators designed a pilot study for the fall 2008 first-time freshmen cohort (Ruiz & Ritze, 2009). The IR and IT offices oversaw the process of collecting data from various sources during this study. By the end of the spring 2009 early advisement period, 2,000 more students had registered. Retention by the spring 2009 semester increased 4%. In informal interviews, collaborators received positive feedback from some departmental chairs regarding the information made available to them via Web reports, including grade distribution, class rosters, and course performance reports. Through a student survey that was collected at this time, the web portal had the highest student satisfaction ratings of all services evaluated (3.2 on a four-point scale).

Efforts to establish a data-information continuum at our college were not always well received. In less formal communications with certain faculty and administrative staff, collaborators became aware that not everyone valued using data and information in decision making. Petrides and Nodine (2003) remind us that it is individuals rather than knowledge systems that manage the knowledge. Resistance was manifested by in the absence of progress grades for certain faculty in the information system. This made it difficult for collaborators to identify what, if any, early intervention strategies students in these instructors' classes could benefit from.

Phase V: Toward Establishing the First-Year Program

Despite the promising integration of KM into the college's efforts to improve student outcomes, the college's retention rate declined in 2010. The Executive Council responded to this decline by naming the freshman year experience as a strategic priority in an effort to increase the rates of student success and completion. To begin to address this multifaceted goal, the college engaged in the Foundations of Excellence self-study process during 2010–2011. Primary collaborators were drawn from Academic

Affairs, Student Development, and Institutional Research. To better understand the needs of freshmen and how to improve their outcomes, collaborators engaged each section of the campus community through multiple discussion formats. One committee used OIR analysis to prioritize the factors that contribute to students' lack of success and drafted concomitant recommendations. In coordination with these, another committee redesigned the existing freshmen seminar as embedded in a wider freshman year experience.

Effective leadership and the support of the president and acting vice president for Academic Affairs facilitated the efficient and productive knowledge transfer between these committees. It is from this significant knowledge base that collaborators drew in designing the first-year experience.

Development of a First-Year Program: Culmination of Knowledge Management Practice Through Collaboration

The development of our new first-year program represents a culmination of our college's KM resources and processes through collaboration and technological innovation. The FYP came about as a result of the recommendations emerging from the Foundations of Excellence (FoE) self-study in 2010–2011. Consistent with findings from institutional research and literature reviews, recommendations addressed improving pedagogy and academic supports, curricular organization, and institutional organization. These recommendations focused intently on creating an impact on students in their first year in a manner that also attended to the wider context of student dispositions and backgrounds. The FoE self-study and the development of the FYP thereafter benefited greatly from the growing knowledge management resources at our college. The growing familiarity of knowledge processes meant that staff and faculty across the college felt more empowered to participate in the self-study process. The first-year seminar helped grow a web of connections between administrative offices and divisions while also integrating faculty to collaborate and interact to improve student success and progress in the first year and beyond. In addition, actionable knowledge indicators already integrated in the knowledge management systems were employed in the design of assessments. All along, college executives strongly supported the first-year initiative as collaborators designed and implemented first-year programming to carry out the FoE recommendations.

The first-year program model encompassed the following goals:

- Supporting student engagement in cocurricular activities.
- Improving advisement of first-semester students.
- Tracking student performance in the first year more closely.
- Supporting students in class with peer mentors.

The organizational structure of the first-year program matched these goals step by step. The first-year seminar replaced an existing college orientation course (a single-credit, two-hour course combining college orientation activities) with a format that introduces academic content through college-level assignments. Faculty members across multiple disciplines teach this course with embedded peer mentors and advisers in each section.

FYS creates a learning environment in which instructors, peer mentors, and advisers work together to support student learning in and outside of the classroom. The team felt that it was important to create mechanisms to identify underperforming students who could then be approached. It also capitalizes on data and information available in the KMS. FYS management, including the program director and the assistant, provides information about the academic progress of students to FYS team members. For example, daily attendance, progress grades, and midterm grades make it possible for faculty and advisers to follow up with struggling and absentee students.

Our FYS is innovative in that it creates an opportunity for faculty to gain experience with this unique academic format, which draws on active, cooperative, and inductive teaching strategies (Wach, Legasa, & Ritze, 2013). Faculty members participate in a comprehensive development program that prepares them to engage students in applied learning techniques that help students develop the disposition, academic habits, and general education skills that will prepare them to succeed in all college classes. In this manner, the first-year seminar is a low-stakes opportunity to try on new teaching styles and exchange ideas with other faculty about teaching. Our working hypothesis is that what works for first-semester students through this format will work for all students. Due to the exploratory and collaborative way in which the course was developed, the FYS team referred to it as a "hatching experience" (Wach et al., 2013). Therefore, the first-year seminar is a learning environment not only for students but also for faculty. The hope is that faculty will begin to employ these strategies in their disciplinary courses.

Engaging and extending the data-information-knowledge continuum is also the clear focus of the first-year program. The program team made it clear in their statement to the collaborators that "the FYS program is transparent, open to investigation, experimentation, and assessment. We want to know what works; if it doesn't work, we will change it" (Wach et al., 2013). To this end, the first-year program team has been collaborating with OIR since the implementation of the program. OIR has implemented an ongoing, multifaceted formative evaluation process to inform ongoing program changes and improvements using interviews, surveys, and observation. Findings are strategically communicated with the FYS team members.

The college has offered the revised first-year seminar in the context of the larger first-year program for three semesters. For the most recent first-year cohort (fall 2012), the one-semester retention rate for FYS takers is 85%, or 6% greater than other freshmen who did not take this course. Following the fall 2012 semester, FYS students earned an average of 6.6 credits and a GPA of 2.29, compared with an average of 3.6 credits and a GPA of 1.60 for students in the traditional freshman seminar course. Currently, 40% of the college's first-year students enrolled in this course as of fall 2013. The college recently secured a grant to facilitate a formative evaluation process to be conducted by outside evaluators. The purpose of this evaluation is to identify best practices generated through the FYP that can be used to improve services and educational experiences for all first-year students.

Conclusion

Engaging in knowledge management practices grew out of the college's need to improve student performance outcomes. Paired with strong collaboration, utilization of IT resources, and the leadership of the associate dean for Institutional Research, knowledge management practices were implemented at our college in five phases. A common knowledge base was created iteratively throughout these phases and became central to the college's prioritization of students' first-year experiences, primarily through a revamped first-year seminar. Based on the results of a preliminary evaluation, the seminar had a promising impact on students' grades, earning of course credits, and retention.

Having witnessed firsthand the value of collaboration and mutual sharing of valuable explicit and tacit knowledge, our goal is now to introduce the value of knowledge management practices to the entire college community.

Recommendations

The emergence of a critical issue facing a college is an excellent opportunity to establish habits of collaboration and knowledge management. College leaders should seize upon these opportunities to bring together departments that do not have a history of working collaboratively so that they may work toward addressing a common issue.

Start with small, collaborative groups, as they are most effective in the early stages of development. Then work on including others in phases.

Differences between data, information, and knowledge should be explained clearly during collaboration. To facilitate this, Institutional Research, Assessment, IT, and other departments that work with a college's data must be given the role of information agent. Members of these departments should sit at the same table with collaborators to go over what the data mean (i.e., to create information). It is important to remember that only when a meaning is given to information can it be converted to action.

Executives and other change agents at the college should support the management of knowledge. They should support and facilitate data and information sharing, as well as investments in data and information resources recommended by staff who actively deal with data. They should also provide opportunities for staff to learn about and engage directly in KM practices and interact with information systems that provide actionable data.

Consider offering incentives for faculty and staff to collaborate on projects. Offer release time to work on projects. Recognize faculty and staff for work that is well done. Applying knowledge is as important as creating knowledge. Identify the obstacles that specific units may encounter in contributing to the knowledge base or acting on available knowledge. Support should be provided to help staff in these units overcome these obstacles through resources, professional development, and training.

References

Alavi, M., & Leidner, D. E. (1999). Knowledge management systems: Issues, challenges, and benefits. *Communications of the Association for Information Systems, 1*, 1–25.

Alavi, M., & Leidner, D. E. (2001). Review: Knowledge management and knowledge management systems. *MIS Quarterly, 25*(1), 109–132.

Chu, W. K., Wang, M., & Yuen, A. H. (2011). Implementing knowledge management in school environment: Teachers' perception. *Knowledge Management & E-Learning: An International Journal (KM&EL), 3*(2), 139–152.

Hizmetli, H., & Ritze, N. (2010, May). *Sharing keys for community college student success: Use of knowledge management to inform a student success effort.* Paper presented at the meeting the Association for Institutional Research, Chicago, IL.

Petrides, L. A., & Nodine, T. R. (2003). *Knowledge management in education: Defining the landscape* (Report). Half Moon Bay, CA: Institute for the Study of Knowledge Management in Education.

Ruiz, E., & Ritze, N. (2003, November). *Facilitating a knowledge-empowered community.* Symposium conducted at the meeting of the Executive Council of Bronx Community College, Bronx, NY.

Ruiz, E., & Ritze, N. (2009, December). *Systematizing information-driven electronic tools and communication systems.* Paper presented at the conference of CUNY Information Technology, New York, NY.

Sedziuviene, N., & Vveinhardt, J. (2009). The paradigm of knowledge management in higher educational institutions. *Inzinerine Ekonomika-Engineering Economics, 20*(5), 79–90.

Wach, H., Legasa, F., & Ritze, N. (2013, March). *Creating a scalable sustainable first year success program.* Symposium conducted at the meeting of the Executive Council of Bronx Community College, Bronx, NY.

HANDAN HIZMETLI is the assistant director of Institutional Research and Planning at Bronx Community College (CUNY).

6

Student affairs and information technology have opportunities to partner in order to increase student satisfaction and retention rates and to assist institutions to comply with federal educational regulations. This chapter contains four examples of emerging best practices and future initiatives including: (a) the admissions pipeline, (b) smart-device application, (c) customized educational planning, and (d) the compliance of financial aid programs.

Student Affairs and Information Technology: Collaborating in the Cloud

Peter Reyes Barbatis

Several studies have examined collaborative initiatives between academic and student affairs designed to integrate curricular and cocurricular experiences with a focus on student learning (Bioland, Stamatakos, & Rogers, 1996; Hyman, 1995; Schroeder & Hurst, 1996). There has been a great emphasis on the first-year experience with increased accountability to raise retention and graduation rates. Instructional departments and student services have begun to create partnerships to remove barriers and work seamlessly. Institutions can no longer allow traditional divisions to exist given the many legislative and mandates from accrediting bodies to include the review of the general education curriculum, assessment of student learning outcomes, and preparation of students for postdegree employment. Hence, student affairs and academic affairs need to work closely together to fulfill the institutional mission and improve college experiences for students (Hyman, 1995; Kuh, 1996).

To date, little research has been done to examine the relationship between student services and other divisions, specifically information technology (IT). Colleges' technological infrastructures have evolved significantly since the late 1990s, as they prepared for Y2K. At the time, the primary concern was to ensure records could be safely accessed in the new millennium. Technology in student services mainly consisted of touchtone phone registration and rudimentary web pages featuring information describing department functions, hours of operation, and building locations. Colleges were considered progressive if forms were made available for

NEW DIRECTIONS FOR COMMUNITY COLLEGES, no. 165, Spring 2014 © 2014 Wiley Periodicals, Inc.
Published online in Wiley Online Library (wileyonlinelibrary.com) • DOI: 10.1002/cc.20091

students to download and print. However, as the popularity and usage of the Internet expanded, so did expectations from students who preferred to use the technology for real-time course registration, grades and transcript access, degree audits, and payment of tuition. Initially, colleges were concerned that students did not have access to the Internet, so they created labs in career centers and registration areas for student use.

However, with rapid technological advances over the past five years, campuses have had to deal with more pressing issues, including the establishment of sufficient Wi-Fi access across campus and of more distance-learning courses. Colleges and universities are quickly attempting to join a Massively Open Online Course (MOOC) consortium and become part of an elite group of schools offering their courses to students around the world (Azevedo, 2012). The American Council on Education has agreed to review 5–10 free online courses offered through Coursera and may recommend that other colleges grant credit for them. It has been argued that these courses may be the next generation of Advanced Placement (AP) credit (Young, 2012).

Today's students expect to be able to rate their colleges on how well they are able to access information and transact with student services via smart devices such as smartphones and tablet computers. Therefore, it is imperative that student affairs develops a strong partnership with information technology.

Needs Analysis

Enrollment is beginning to decline across the nation's college campuses (Johnson, 2011; Marcus, 2012). After climbing almost 22% since 2007, community college enrollment declined 1% in 2012 (Marcus, 2012). While some argue that the decline stems from an improving economy, fewer layoffs, and a drop in the number of high school graduates, institutions must nonetheless compete more aggressively to attract students. Although cost is a factor, students may choose a much more expensive school based on an institution's customer service and how effectively the institution communicates with prospects. There is an expectation of a high level of customer service and quick response time. In addition, there is an emphasis on the completion agenda.

Institutions are beginning to become more prescriptive in their programs of study and mandate certain expectations to include the sequence of courses, the number of credit hours a student takes, and embedded support services. At the same time, students are becoming more technologically savvy. In 2005, Educause, through its Center for Applied Research, found that 96% of college students surveyed indicated that they owned at least one computer (Kiernan, 2005). Computers aren't the only form of technology common in students' lives. When asked whether they owned a desktop computer, laptop, personal digital assistant, smartphone, cell phone, music device, or wireless adapter, students reported owning an average of three

NEW DIRECTIONS FOR COMMUNITY COLLEGES • DOI: 10.1002/cc

such devices (Kiernan, 2005). As a result of higher expectations among students and increased competition among institutions to attract and retain students, institutions must continually employ technology to create a positive experience for students and provide support service staff with the requisite tools to enhance job performance and effectiveness.

Emerging and Promising Practices

Technological advancements may help contribute to higher student satisfaction and retention rates (Kiernan, 2005) and to assisting institutions in complying with federal regulations. Four examples of emerging best practices and future initiatives to be discussed here include: (a) the admissions pipeline, (b) smart-device applications, (c) customized educational planning, and (d) financial aid program compliance.

The Admissions Pipeline.   Digitally savvy students expect to be able to get information when they need it, in real time. It is counterproductive to provide too many directions at once. Students want to know: "What do I need to do next?" This is illustrated by the creation of the admissions pipeline. Community colleges realize that they lose a significant percentage of students between the initial application process and the payment of tuition. During each step of enrollment, there are groups of students who do not complete next steps, such as residency, placement testing, orientation, registration, and payment. At some institutions, this number may be as high as 60%.

Since these "lost" students are not accounted for in records pertaining to, for example, collected tuition and fees or FTE appropriations, the work of the student affairs office is often unaccounted for. Further, financial aid offices may include students who list particular institutions on their FAFSA and subsequently do not attend. Traditionally, proprietary schools communicate with their applicants efficiently. However, many two-year colleges have difficulty communicating with newly admitted students and communicating next steps in their admissions process, particularly when freshman and transfer classes exceed 2,000 students per term. In fall 2012, Palm Beach State College, in Lake Worth, Florida, instituted an admissions pipeline whereby the student services and IT departments identified a series of enrollment milestones to indicate certain factors that prevent a student from continuing to the next phase of admission. These included the following:

- Proof of residency.
- Transient students submitting approved courses from their home institutions.
- Students requiring placement testing.
- Dual-enrollment students who need high school approval.
- Students required to attend orientation or an educational planning session.

- Students qualified to register.
- Students who still owe tuition or fees.

For each enrollment milestone, a refreshed list of prospective students' names, phone numbers, mailing addresses, and email addresses was created and divided by campus. The district office, on a weekly basis, reminded students via text messaging, "robo calls," or e-mail of next steps. Campus staff called individual applicants who had completed the admissions process, tested and attended orientation, and needed only to register. The college found that very few students opted out of receiving the communication, and a great majority opted for text messages rather than e-mail. The greatest challenge was ensuring that text messages accurately communicated a message in fewer than 160 characters. As a result of this effort, there was a 5% increase in enrollment for first-time college students as compared to the previous fall semester (Palm Beach State College, 2012).

These data allowed the college to plan more effectively. We were able to determine how many new student orientations were needed and to project the number of developmental courses and first-level English and mathematics courses needed for incoming students. A significant problem for institutions is matching course advisement with the number of actual classroom seats available. Many students who cannot find classes they want simply do not enroll.

For this initiative to succeed, institutions must develop a workflow of the necessary steps to enrollment and subsequently capture these data elements to identify the type of student (first time in college, transfer, transient, dual enrollment) and their status in the admissions process. For example, many colleges require that students have placement test scores, and that they register for and complete new student orientation and educational planning. This information must be collected and retrieved to determine these students' status. Finally, institutions must have the appropriate contact information, such as cell phone numbers, to communicate with students.

Smart-Device Applications.   Another technological initiative is the design of smart-device applications or "apps." To put the phenomenon in perspective, 17.4 million smart devices, including Apple's iPhone and iPad, Samsung's Galaxy, and Amazon's Kindle Fire, were in use as of December 25, 2012, compared to 6.8 million one year earlier (Farago, 2012). Further, 328 million apps had been downloaded as of December 25, 2012 (Farago, 2012). It is clear that students possess and extensively use their smart devices and download new applications each day. As a result, many students will develop relationships with the college through a smart device. The application should not just mirror what students can do online, but have several additional tools to help them. One is a GPS, which can provide students with directions to classes and buildings as part of their class schedules. Despite the fact that many institutions may include a campus tour as part of their new student orientation program, many students will not pay careful attention, as they have not yet registered for classes, thus making the locations of the buildings not yet relevant, for example.

One of the greatest challenges many institutions face is answering the phones during peak registration periods. Many of these phone calls are in regard to students' financial aid status. Another component of the smart-device application is a financial aid tracker to let students know where they are in the application process. Students who are chosen for verification can be advised of missing documents and expected date of packaging. In addition, weekly reminders could pop up on their phones with dates and announcements. Finally, many institutions struggle with the last day of attendance to calculate the refund amount due to the federal government. Smart devices could be used to this end having students "check in" as a way of capturing attendance when they enter the class.

Customized Educational Plan.   Another initiative in which student affairs needs the support of information technology is educational planning. Students who know the exact courses they need to take and in which sequence will more likely continue in school and fulfill the completion agenda (Lau, 2003). Ideally, all students should tentatively declare a major during first semester, indicate their intended transfer institution, specify whether they plan to attend full-time or part-time, and enroll for summer sessions. These parameters generate a four- to eight-semester plan of sequenced courses. Every term, this should automatically populate a student's "shopping list" when he or she registers for classes. To ensure financial aid compliance, students should be warned if they are taking classes outside their program of study. This helps students to stay on track, and decreases time to degree, but also helps academic affairs forecast the number of course sections needed for each class. Colleges could implement a year-round class schedule and assign the appropriate number of faculty. It is widely known that students will change their majors or that they may not successfully complete each class recorded on their educational plan in the sequence indicated, but the plan can be changed where advisers or counselors provide the support needed. The greater challenge is ensuring that the majors and transfer courses needed remain current by catalog year and appropriately programmed. Information technology cannot accomplish educational planning in the absence of collaboration between academic and student affairs.

Financial Aid Program Objective Course Compliance.   Finally, another example of an initiative where a partnership is needed is program objective course compliance. Federal financial aid requires that students not take classes outside a student's program of study. Institutions must communicate this early to students to ensure they are accountable to financial aid. The comprehensive educational plan may assist with this endeavor; however, as part of the package, students need to review if any of their classes are not related to their major and make informed decisions regarding their major. This customized information needs to be available online, emailed, and texted to the student by the registrar's office.

These are just a few examples of how student affairs and information technology may partner. Future innovations regarding information technology and student support services may include: remote proctoring for online courses, video embedded text messaging, and customized marketing and targeting of support services. In the near future, all of these issues will need to be addressed.

Recommendations

Students expect to receive a full range of student support services via smart devices. All of these initiatives require an inclusion of information technology. It is imperative that student affairs professionals develop a relationship with IT leaders in order to share the institution's vision and purpose. Student affairs has an obligation to illustrate how IT, which is removed from day-to-day interaction with students, can support and enhance the student experience; together, they can address challenges. It is important that we mutually understand our missions and be inclusive. Student affairs must become better acquainted with IT acronyms such as API (application programming interface), power-pivot tables, and SQL (structured query language). Student affairs leaders should consider attending the Educause conference and subscribing to its periodicals to keep abreast of innovations and to generate ideas for future initiatives. IT should also be present during peak registration to assist students and staff. Student affairs leaders should ask for help from IT in solving challenges that arise. It is important to realize that there are many priorities placed on IT, including the updating of equipment, negotiation of software purchases, and departmental projects from colleagues in human resources, payroll, and academic affairs (distance learning, in particular); however, student affairs activities should be considered integral to the welfare of the institution. Perhaps we can request to serve on the advisory committee that establishes priorities. As a colleague recently stated in reference to student affairs and information technology, "Touchy feely has to create a partnership with the geek and realize it's what keeps the school going forward."

Conclusion

The partnership between student affairs and information technology does not suggest that there is a need for less student affairs staffing or that personal contact has become obsolete. Students indicate that they desire a balance between technology and human touch (Kiernan, 2005). Students cite convenience as the primary benefit in the use of technology (Kiernan, 2005). As a result, student affairs should focus more intently on developing and fostering relationships with students as they focus on career development, securing jobs, and completing cocurricular programs. We need to differentiate between transactional support and holistic development. Institutions should utilize technology for the former and employ direct human contact for the latter.

Student affairs is well positioned for partnership. Traditionally, we have created relationships with many campus constituents, including institutional research, facilities, and academic affairs. Our profession understands the importance of developing relationships and facilitation. Change may be threatening and challenging yet can be achieved if we build trust and openness, and appreciate diverse viewpoints. Our primary intent should be not only to bridge boundaries in order to create a seamless experience for our students but also to provide our staff with the necessary tools to do their jobs more effectively. We are all critical stakeholders in student success.

References

Azevedo, A. (2012, September 26). In colleges' rush to try MOOC's, faculty are not always in the conversation. *Chronicle of Higher Education, 59*(6), A22. Retrieved from http://chronicle.com/article/In-Colleges-Rush-to-Try/134692/

Bioland, P. A., Stamatakos, L. C., & Rogers, R. R. (1996). Redirecting the role of student affairs to focus on student learning. *Journal of College Student Development, 37*(2), 217–226.

Farago, P. (2012, December 27). Christmas 2012 shatters more smart device and app download records. *Flurry Blog.* Retrieved from http://blog.flurry.com/bid/92719 /Christmas-2012-Shatters-More-Smart-Device-and-App-Download-Records

Hyman, R. (1995). Creating campus partnerships for student success. *College & University, 71*(2), 2–8.

Johnson, L. (2011, October 18). Community college enrollments slow after years of growth. *Chronicle of Higher Education.* Retrieved from http://chronicle.com/article /Community-College-Enrollments/129462/

Kiernan, V. (2005, November 25). Students desire a balance of technological and human contact, survey suggests. *Chronicle of Higher Education, 52*(14), A41. Retrieved from http://chronicle.com/article/Students-Desire-a-Balance-of/11687/

Kuh, G. D. (1996). Guiding principles for creating seamless learning environments for undergraduates. *Journal of College Student Development, 37*(2), 135–148.

Lau, L. (2003). Institutional factors affecting student retention. *Education, 124*(1), 126–136.

Marcus, J. (2012, May 31). College enrollment shows signs of slowing. *The Hechinger Report.* Retrieved from http://hechingerreport.org/content/college-enrollment-shows -signs-of-slowing_8688/

Palm Beach State College. (2012). *Beginning of term student database frequency analysis of demographic record data elements* [Data file]. Lake Worth, FL: Author.

Schroeder, C. S., & Hurst, J. C. (1996). Designing learning environments that integrate curricular and cocurricular experiences. *Journal of College Student Development, 37*(2), 174–181.

Young, J. R. (2012, November 13). American Council on Education may recommend some Coursera offerings for college credit. *Chronicle of Higher Education, 59*(13), A23. Retrieved from http://chronicle.com/article/MOOCs-Take-a-Major-Step/135750/

PETER REYES BARBATIS *is the vice president for Student Services/Enrollment Management at Palm Beach State College in Lake Worth, Florida.*

NEW DIRECTIONS FOR COMMUNITY COLLEGES • DOI: 10.1002/cc

7

This chapter examines the roles, reasons, facilitators, and challenges of chief executive, academic, and student affairs officers in internationalizing the community college student experience.

The Role of Key Administrators in Internationalizing the Community College Student Experience

Ronald D. Opp, Penny Poplin Gosetti

Community colleges in America are under increasing pressure to internationalize the student experience to better prepare students to live and work in a global economy. The calls for internationalizing the community college stem from a variety of sources, including from both of the major community college organizations—the American Association of Community Colleges and the American Community College Trustees, which published the *Joint Statement on the Role of Community Colleges in International Education* (AACC/ACCT, 2006). In this joint statement, they argued "community colleges should develop strategic plans for global awareness and competence that respond to the needs of the community's learners, businesses, and institutions" (para. 1). The call to action by these major community college organizations was reinforced the following year in a *New Directions for Community Colleges* article by two international education scholars, Raby and Valeau (2007), in which they argued that "without international education in community colleges, many students would not have the chance to expand their understanding of the global world or change their perceptions and attitudes about global relationships" (p. 10). This same call to action was reinforced in a recent *New Directions for Community Colleges* article by two other international education scholars, Treat and Hagedorn (2013), who argued that "U.S. community colleges, and the community college model in general, are poised to play a crucial role in the evolving global economic, social, and educational environment, should we meet the challenge" (p. 6). Clearly, a growing call for action is coming from both community college organizations and scholars of community college internationalization.

NEW DIRECTIONS FOR COMMUNITY COLLEGES, no. 165, Spring 2014 © 2014 Wiley Periodicals, Inc.
Published online in Wiley Online Library (wileyonlinelibrary.com) • DOI: 10.1002/cc.20092

The Current Status of Internationalization in Community Colleges

Despite these growing calls for internationalization, a series of reports from the American Council on Education stretching back a decade provides evidence that the community college sector lags behind other sectors of higher education in this arena. The American Council on Education has published a series of *Mapping Internationalization on U.S. Campuses* reports that examined internationalization policies and practices by Carnegie Classification of Institutions of Higher Education (see, e.g., Center for Internationalization and Global Engagement [CIGE], 2012; Green, Luu, & Burris, 2008). In the most recent 2012 report, the Center for Internationalization and Global Engagement (CIGE) noted, "while associate institutions have made progress in some areas, their overall levels of internationalization are still below those of institutions in other sectors" (p. 24). Given that approximately 40% of American undergraduates attend this sector, the report argued that higher education policy makers and researchers should consider devoting more study to identifying successful internationalization strategies and models emerging from this sector.

The renewed call for attention to internationalization in the community college sector is occurring alongside a growing call for more comprehensive internationalization in all higher education institutions (Hill & Green, 2008). "*Comprehensive internationalization* describes a more ambitious and intentional approach, in which internationalization ultimately pervades the institution, affecting a broad spectrum of people, policies and programs as well as institutional culture" (Hill & Green, 2008, p. vii). The Community Colleges for International Development (CCID) has recently developed a *Framework for Comprehensive Internationalization*, which attempts to describe the phases that a community college moves through in its journey toward comprehensive internationalization (Bissonette & Woodin, 2013). The phases of this framework describe a continuum that ranges from community colleges that are not yet "actively pursuing internationalization programming" (p. 16) to those where "pervasive and omnipresent global perspectives touch every student, staff member, and faculty member at a comprehensively internationalized community college" (p. 17). The development of this internationalization framework allows community colleges to begin to conduct self-audits that determine what phase they are in, and how their internationalization progress compares with that of other community colleges. Thus, the internationalization agenda is experiencing not only more attention from international education scholars but also a new emphasis on moving the agenda toward transforming the community college through *comprehensive internationalization*.

Given this growing focus on the internationalization agenda, community college practitioners may wonder who is responsible for taking the lead in promoting this agenda. On this point, a consensus is growing that not only the entire campus needs to be involved in comprehensive internationalization but also some key administrators on the community college campus need to take leadership roles (Hudzik & McCarthy, 2012).

Moving Forward the Internationalization Agenda

Three key administrators are crucial to the internationalization agenda, including the chief executive officer (CEO), the chief academic officer (CAO), and the chief student affairs officer (CSAO). We have conducted national surveys over the last three years with these three administrator groups to document their views about and roles in internationalizing the community college student experience. The results from these surveys and their implications for moving forward the internationalization agenda can be found in the sections that follow.

Roles of Key Administrators in Supporting Internationalization. All three administrative groups were asked about their personal involvement in internationalization on their campuses. More than a quarter of the CEOs reported being very involved, followed by one sixth of the CAOs, and only one eighth of the CSAOs. The responses of these three groups to this question demonstrate that the majority of these administrators are not personally involved in internationalization on their campuses.

As noted earlier, international education scholars have argued that the involvement of key administrators is critical to the success of the internationalization agenda. In addition to the financial, human, and symbolic support, these administrative groups provide internationalization initiatives; one could also argue that their appreciation and understanding of the value and importance of internationalization might be enhanced if they were personally involved.

Key administrators have different, but complementary roles in moving forward comprehensive internationalization. The president is responsible for articulating the vision for international education, both to the campus community and to the board of trustees and external stakeholder groups. Once this vision has been articulated, it is the president's role to provide the resources necessary to professionally develop and support the campus leadership involved in internationalization, to engage internal and external stakeholder groups in discussions about its benefits, and to make sure that information about international education activities and opportunities is disseminated.

The CAO plays a complementary role to that of the president, but with a primary focus on faculty affairs and curriculum. The primary internationalization roles of the CAO include such activities as working with faculty to integrate global perspectives into general education curriculum, providing resources for faculty to lead study abroad programs, and in joining consortia, like CCID, or the California Colleges for International Education (CCIE), to enhance international study capabilities.

NEW DIRECTIONS FOR COMMUNITY COLLEGES • DOI: 10.1002/cc

The CSAO plays another vital, but complementary role to that of the CAO in comprehensive internationalization. The CSAO is responsible for such internationalization activities as administering and providing resources for support services to international students, sponsoring international activities and events on campus, and developing on-campus programs to integrate socially domestic and international students. Each of the roles these key administrators play in internationalizing the student experience complements one another, and all are essential in moving the college toward comprehensive internationalization.

Given the importance of administrative involvement noted in the literature, several possible strategies for advancing comprehensive internationalization emerge. First, a strong case can be made for including prior experience and/or interest in internationalization in the recruitment of key community college administrators on campus (Hudzik & McCarthy, 2012). A similar strategy has been suggested for the recruitment of community college faculty (CIGE, 2012). Adding such criteria to administrative job announcements demonstrates the commitment of the college to comprehensive internationalization. For those administrators hired without international experiences, but with an expressed interest in internationalization, presidents need to find the time and the resources necessary to provide professional development for these individuals. This professional development might include attendance at international education conferences, such as CCID, or NAFSA: Association for International Educators annual international conferences, where community college administrators can share with one another promising policies and practices in internationalizing community colleges.

One might also ask what role the chief international officer (CIO) plays in internationalization efforts in community colleges. The CIGE (2012) report indicates that 56% of community colleges employ a full-time administrator who oversees or coordinates internationalization activities and programs. Brennan and Dellow (2013), however, have suggested, "Too often, community colleges designate a campus president, vice president, dean, or faculty member to manage international education instead of installing a full-time and fully qualified CIO" (p. 34). They argue that internationalization may not receive sufficient attention if it is a shared or an added-on responsibility.

Our national surveys did not specifically ask each of the administrative groups if they had a dedicated, full-time CIO. One might expect that on those community college campuses with a CIO, this administrator plays a vital role in developing and implementing strategies for comprehensive internationalization. Further research is clearly needed on how many community colleges have CIOs, and the roles that they play in comprehensive internationalization.

Reasons for Internationalizing. International education scholars have posited a host of reasons for internationalizing the student experience, including academic, economic, social, and national and foreign policy goals (Hill & Green, 2008). The three administrative groups we examined also emphasized different reasons for internationalizing the community college student experience. The CEOs were most likely to mention the following reasons: globalization is changing the job prospects for the college's students; the ability of college students to work across cultural boundaries is crucial in a global economy; and studying abroad is a life-altering experience for students. The top two reasons presidents mentioned focus on the area of workforce development, which is a community college mission that is often a top priority for them. The importance that presidents place on workforce development no doubt, in part, stems from the role that they play in articulating the workforce and economic development missions of their colleges to business and industry groups typically represented on the board of trustees, and to external stakeholder groups.

The CAOs and the CSAOs are more likely than presidents to have to articulate comprehensive internationalization to internal audiences, including faculty and student groups. Because CAOs interact on a regular basis with faculty, and have oversight for the curriculum and student learning outcomes, their reasons for internationalization fell primarily in the educational category. These reasons included that internationalization promotes global awareness in students, that international diversity enriches classroom discussion, and that internationalization helps develop attitudes of tolerance and understanding of different cultures. Their reasons for internationalization deal with pedagogy and the assessment of student learning outcomes, areas for which CAOs have primary responsibility.

The CSAOs agreed with CAOs about the importance of internationalization for promoting global awareness, but their reasons for internationalization tended to focus on out-of-the-classroom affective outcomes and environments, such as helping students develop attitudes of tolerance and understanding of different cultures and creating inclusive campus environments welcoming to international students. These affective outcomes and campus climate issues are areas often seen as the primary responsibility of the CSAO. Although these three administrative groups often work with different internal and external stakeholder groups, they all need to appreciate and be able to articulate the value and importance of internationalization to the stakeholder groups with whom the college interacts.

Facilitators of Internationalization. The different administrative groups are also likely to agree that different components of the college campus are facilitators of internationalization. The CEO group is most likely to agree that key internationalization facilitators include a campus culture that supports international activities, a board of trustees that supports internationalization, and the attractiveness of the college to international students. While international education scholars have argued that community colleges sometimes struggle to have their boards understand the value of internationalization, they also have emphasized the essential role that boards of trustees must play as facilitators of comprehensive internationalization (see, e.g., Bissonette & Woodin, 2013; Hudzik & McCarthy, 2012).

Presidents need to be able to educate board members about the value and importance of internationalization, from both an educational and an economic development perspective. They also need to work with their administrative team to develop a culture on campus that supports internationalization and to create an infrastructure that successfully attracts international students. Creating such an infrastructure might involve examining available options for housing international students, developing appropriate transportation options, and providing international student services and programs, including English as a second language classes, student visa services, and ways to integrate international students into the campus community.

The CAO is more likely than the president to focus on tangible internal supports for internationalization, including making sure that internationalization is part of the college's strategic plan and budget, and that communication systems are in place to keep faculty and students informed about international opportunities. Chief academic officers can use the prominence of internationalization in strategic plans and budgets to justify providing professional development funds for faculty and to help encourage them to lead study abroad programs.

Chief student affairs officers are likely to cite students and student development staff as the key facilitators of internationalization, including student interest in international education, the presence of international students on campus, and the understanding and appreciation of student development staff for the college's internationalization efforts. Chief student affairs officers are perhaps best positioned to understand the importance of students' intrinsic interest in international education, and that interactions between domestic and international students can present powerful opportunities for internationalization.

Addressing the Challenges to Internationalization.   Both CEOs and CAOs agree that work and family responsibilities make it difficult for students on their campuses to study abroad. In particular, CAOs are concerned about the lack of adequate staff and infrastructure for internationalization, and the lack of adequate funding for international travel. Presidents also mentioned that recent cuts in state funding have exacerbated the challenge of funding their colleges' international activities, and that their colleges have a challenge to provide international students with access to support services.

The *Mapping Internationalization* reports from ACE have documented how the community college sector has made progress in internationalization, but the 2012 report (CIGE, 2012) notes that it still lags behind other sectors in higher education in areas such as the percentage of community colleges with campus-wide internationalization plans, formal assessment of their internationalization efforts, specific scholarships for education abroad, and campus-wide policies or guidelines for partnerships. Community college administrators may look at the funding and infrastructure challenges, and conclude that it will be difficult to move their campuses toward comprehensive internationalization. Making progress on internationalization, despite these fiscal and infrastructure constraints, may be particularly difficult for rural community colleges. Harder (2011) found in her research that rural community colleges are experiencing significantly less internationalization than their urban or suburban counterparts.

The distinctive challenges presented by internationalization may require that community colleges partner with neighboring higher education institutions to promote a regional approach to internationalization. Recent data indicate that just 15% of two-year institutions fund travel to recruit students abroad (CIGE, 2012). Perhaps two-year colleges can work with neighboring four-year colleges to recruit international students for both institutions. As an example, representatives from Kirkwood Community College travel with admissions representatives from the University of Iowa when recruiting students internationally. Both institutions have worked to build joint degree programs so that international students can start at Kirkwood Community College knowing that they have a specific pathway to a university degree at the University of Iowa (Clark, 2012). Community colleges have several marketing advantages in developing these partnerships with universities, in that their tuition is typically much less than a four-year university, their class sizes tend to be smaller, and the university pathways can be personalized to the degree aspirations of the student.

Another avenue to pursue is to ensure that global experiences and internationalization training are provided in the community college leadership training programs that are preparing the next generation of community college leaders. If we want to ensure the next generation of community college leaders has an appreciation for and a deep understanding of the importance of internationalization, then faculty in community college leadership training programs must provide their students with global experiences and opportunities to learn how to internationalize the community college student experience.

Conclusions

International education scholars make strong arguments that comprehensive internationalization is now "an institutional imperative, not just a desirable possibility" (Hudzik & McCarthy, 2012, p. iv). Internationalizing the community college student experience is becoming ever more important as the world becomes increasingly "flat," and the economy becomes increasingly more global. We need to prepare a generation of community college leaders who have global experiences and a deep appreciation for the value and importance of internationalization. In particular, the CEOs, the CAOs, and the CSAOs in community colleges need to understand their individual and collective roles, reasons, facilitators, and challenges to comprehensive internationalization. Most importantly, if community college administrators are to be successful in moving their colleges toward comprehensive internationalization, they need to be personally involved in internationalizing the community college student experience. Working together with faculty and students, these key administrators can help create a culture and build an infrastructure for comprehensive internationalization on their campuses.

References

AACC/ACCT. (2006). *AACC/ACCT joint statement on the role of community colleges in international education.* Retrieved from http://www.aacc .nche.edu/About/Positions/Pages/ps10012006.aspx

Bissonette, B., & Woodin, S. (2013). Building support for internationalization through institutional assessment and leadership engagement. In T. Treat & L. S. Hagedorn (Eds.), *New Directions for Community Colleges: No. 161. The community college in a global context* (pp. 11–26). San Francisco, CA: Jossey-Bass.

Brennan, M., & Dellow, D. A. (2013). International students as a resource for achieving comprehensive internationalization. In T. Treat & L. S. Hagedorn (Eds.), *New Directions for Community Colleges: No. 161. The community college in a global context* (pp. 27–37). San Francisco, CA: Jossey-Bass.

Center for Internationalization and Global Engagement (CIGE). (2012). *Mapping internationalization on U.S. campuses: 2012 edition.* Washington, DC: American Council on Education.

Clark, N. (2012). Internationalizing the community college campus. *World Education News and Reviews.* Retrieved from http://wenr.wes.org/2012/10/wenr -october-2012-internationalizing-the-community-college-campus/

Green, M., Luu, D. T., & Burris, B. (2008). *Mapping internationalization on U.S. campuses: 2008 edition.* Washington, DC: American Council on Education.

Harder, N. (2011). Internationalization efforts in United States community colleges: A comparative analysis of urban, suburban, and rural institutions. *Community College Journal of Research and Practice, 35,* 152–164.

Hill, B., & Green, M. (2008). *A guide to internationalization for chief academic officers.* Washington, DC: American Council on Education.

Hudzik, J. K., & McCarthy, J. S. (2012). *Leading comprehensive internationalization: Strategy and tactics for action.* NAFSA: Association of International Educators. Retrieved from http://www.nafsa.org/uploadedFiles/Chez_NAFSA/Resource_Library_Assets /Publications_Library/Leading%20CIZN.pdf

Raby, R. L., & Valeau, E. J. (2007). Community college international education: Looking back to forecast the future. *New Directions for Community Colleges: No. 138.*

International reform efforts and challenges in community colleges (pp. 5–14). San Francisco, CA: Jossey-Bass.

Treat, T., & Hagedorn, L. S. (2013). Resituating the community college in a global context. In T. Treat & L. S. Hagedorn (Eds.), *New Directions for Community Colleges: No. 161. The community college in a global context* (pp. 5–9). San Francisco, CA: Jossey-Bass.

RONALD D. OPP *is an associate professor and doctoral coordinator of the Higher Education Program at the University of Toledo.*

PENNY POPLIN GOSETTI *is the dean of the Judith Herb College of Education and an associate professor in the Higher Education Program at the University of Toledo.*

8

The nonprofit consortium California Colleges for International Education (CCIE) is a working example of how a formal association involving community colleges uses collaboration to achieve a fundamental goal of increasing student awareness of international issues through study abroad programs. For over 30 years, CCIE members have worked together to advocate internationalization and to sustain organized efforts that share best practices and forge partnerships between colleges within a state system. CCIE member colleges have worked together to advocate and initiate the growth of study abroad programs through institutional collaborations.

Collaboration: Use of Consortia to Promote International Education

Rosalind Latiner Raby, Donald R. Culton, Edward J. Valeau

California Colleges for International Education (CCIE) is a nationally recognized nonprofit advocacy organization that advances international education for community college students. For over 30 years, CCIE has advocated student learning by managing a clearinghouse that shares best practices about how collaborative ventures are built. Collaboration in this context is demonstrated through alliances between departments within colleges as well as through partnerships between colleges in the California state education system. Relationships that come to fruition often continue to exist over future decades, at times during challenging political and economic periods.

Community College international education programs aim to connect students, faculty, and members of local communities with people in foreign cultures. The goal is to "accelerate knowledge about and encourage cross-cultural communication to enhance culture, ethnic, class and gender relationships among divergent groups" (Raby & Valeau, 2007, p. 6). College graduates now require proficiency to navigate the complexities of the modern world. Recent studies confirm the academic and personal benefits of exposure to cultures in other countries.

International education within community colleges has existed for nearly 50 years, yet it remains a peripheral activity despite having received state and national fiscal support (Raby, 2007). Yet this support has been sporadic and has required the assistance of CCIE. Specifically, CCIE member colleges work together to advocate and initiate programmatic and institutional change, and to maintain cross-sector and statewide institutional collaborations to advance international exchange.

Background

International education has appeared in the community college classroom in various ways. Faculty teach students about the world, introduce foreign languages and classical European music, and instruct students about international business. A movement toward internationalization in education began in the early 1970s when a group of interested faculty at a public college in California added global education to augment their classes. Later, students participated in college-sponsored study abroad programs for college credit. By the mid-1970s, colleges began to promote study abroad programs as a way to generate revenue. Some colleges advertised these programs by highlighting for students the benefits of traveling abroad. These activities did not require statewide collaboration.

In 1976, California allowed colleges to generate revenue by offering college-level courses abroad. That same year, a group of educators from across the state organized a movement to expand support study abroad programs. They adopted a contract for the California State University (CSU) to partner with third party study abroad contractors. In 1982, they launched an advocacy campaign to inform the State Chancellor's office about the financial and academic benefits of internationalization. CCIE was then established in 1983. What started as a group of 19 member colleges today comprises 86 member colleges (CCIE, 2013).

CCIE was not the only community college collaborative in the early years to support international education. During the 1980s, several national associations supported a growing international education presence at community colleges. These groups sought to advance internationalization with the support of a group of college presidents who were committed to their students having international exposure. While presidential support was always recognized, CCIE also emphasized faculty participation, which served as a catalyst for greater student involvement. CCIE's position is that international education should be accessible for everyone, regardless of college size or income (Raby, 1999).

Collaboration for Advocacy

Advocacy began in 1947 when internationalization was defined in the *Report from the President's Commission on Higher Education* (Zook, 1947) as not being in opposition to local influence as communities are linked between and beyond borders. The current AACC (2012) *Reclaiming the American*

Dream underscores this by stating "it is important that college graduates, wherever their location, be not just *globally competitive* but also *globally competent*, understanding their roles as citizens and workers in an international context" (p. 10). Both documents counter a prevailing and crippling myth that the community college should not be involved in international activities based on a dim view that international students take seats away from local students. Experiences gained from studying abroad are luxuries few community college students can afford, and an internationalized curriculum will not help students obtain jobs. While these arguments are not valid, they exist. CCIE advocacy has been a fundamental reason why these myths have been disputed and challenged within the California community college arena (Raby, 2007).

Since community colleges serve a greater proportion of lower income and minority students than any other postsecondary institution, the open access philosophy is precisely the means that make international knowledge and experience accessible to students who would not otherwise be able to participate. Advocacy emphasizes how internationalization is a way in which California community college administrators, trustees, and policy makers can maintain equitable access because what opportunities benefit four-year college students should also be given to community college students.

CCIE advocacy is targeted at professionals at various levels. To support top-down level change, CCIE has always had presidents on its board and included them in program activities to support institutional change, success, and advocacy. However, CCIE also recognizes that this approach does not always ensure success. For this reason, advocacy has been integrated within staff and faculty development. CCIE understands that without faculty advocates, there are few who will teach an internationalized curriculum, serve on international committees, or lead an education abroad program.

CCIE advocacy is evident as California senior administrators share enthusiastic support of international education, even amid the state economic crisis. One hundred percent of the responding CEOs in the CCIE (2010) survey said that international education does contribute to the success of the college's mission. The following statements illuminate their sentiments: "international education supports our mission and interest in student diversity," while another respondent indicates "students expect preparation to participate in a global society." The connection of international education to specific mission items is also addressed as "global education enriches the teaching/learning process, student life, student engagement, and student growth and development." All of the responding CEOs in this survey acknowledge that the key competencies needed to advance student success are in building international skills obtained through educational programming.

CCIE has collaboratively helped to usher in various changes in California community colleges. In 1985, few colleges had an internationalization agenda, fewer trustees supported internationalization, and there was no support at the statewide level. In 2010, more than half of all California community colleges included the importance of international education in their mission statements (CCIE, 2010). In the 2013–2014 academic year, 36 colleges will offer education abroad programs, which will serve more than half of all U.S. community college students who study abroad. In 2012, 101 colleges had international student programs that were attended by approximately 24,983 international students (NAFSA/IIE, 2013). The longevity of this impact is clear in that about 61% of the CCIE member colleges have supported international education for over 10 years and 18% have supported international education for over 21 years (CCIE, 2013).

Collaboration to Initiate Programmatic and Institutional Change

CCIE plays a central role in the development of new and existing academic programs to support internationalization. The CCIE collaborative strategy includes sharing best practices to guide regulatory policy, communication to expand opportunities for colleges by strengthening partnerships, and programming based on collaboration.

International education at California community colleges grew from a grassroots effort. Initially no regulations existed to define the field. In 1983, CCIE used the Hess (1982) framework to develop the following guidelines to help California community colleges to institutionalize international education: (a) create centrally located offices where students, faculty, and community know where to obtain information on international education; (b) provide staff and operating expenses to support these offices; (c) establish college policy on how to establish programs, define faculty selection, market programs, and adhere to other legal, health, and safety issues affiliated with these programs; and (d) define risk management programs to better serve students and colleges. CCIE membership includes a signed agreement by college presidents to adhere to these guidelines. Today, national associations, such as NAFSA, American Council on Education, and the Forum on Education Abroad, continue to regulate the field, and CCIE redefines these regulations for California community colleges.

Communication is the cornerstone for the CCIE clearinghouse for best practices to help guide new teaching strategies, assessment, and learning practices. As part of its strategic planning, CCIE conducts an annual survey of members and publishes the findings in an annual report to detail the full sweep of international education activities among colleges every year. Even before the advent of the Internet, paper newsletters circulated member institutional best practices. Today, the CCIE web page facilitates an online monthly newsletter that highlights current issues. Without this clearinghouse, some programs would be vulnerable to the loss of institutional support that could impact student learning.

Another example of collaboration is the International Negotiations Modules Project (INMP), a statewide program in which multiple colleges participate in an online internationalizing curriculum simulation. Since 1995, nearly 16 California community colleges partner with community colleges nationwide in a simulation that creates an online classroom community wherein students communicate with students from other classrooms, other disciplines, other colleges, and other geographic locations (Raby, Kaufman, & Rabb, 2012). Faculty develop the curriculum for the simulation and students learn and interact about current events.

Advertising international education abroad programs for students involves sharing program information and schedules in print and online on the CCIE web page. This enables students to get information about any program in California and attend any community college to study abroad. CCIE encourages colleges to work together to design, coordinate, market, share program costs, and accept transfer of college credits. In the early 1990s, a multicollege/district collaboration between Los Angeles Harbor College, Los Angeles Pierce College, and Cypress College created a program for instructors to teach in Cambridge, England. Students could take classes taught by any of the faculty and receive credit from their home institution. Another formalized collaboration is the California Foothills Consortium that has been coordinated by Citrus Community College since 1987. Citrus College provides classes and rotates instructors from member colleges. In this way, each campus can involve as few as one student without the overhead costs affiliated with these programs.

Collaboration on Cross-Sector Statewide Institutional Projects

Higher education in California is built on the California Master Plan, which defines a tri-level system to establish the role of community colleges, California State University, and University of California (UC). Cross-sector statewide projects have existed for decades. In the 1990s, some associations began to link with other institutions to promote international education. CCIE has and continues to represent the community college voice in these associations.

The California Community Colleges Chancellor's Office in Sacramento does not have a staff member whose responsibility is to oversee international education. Since 1985, CCIE has been the primary voice to the Chancellor's Office international education initiatives and programs to bring activities to scale system-wide. This support was formalized with the late 1990s revision of the California Education Code Sec. 297 66010.4.3 (1999–2008), which stated "a primary mission of the California Community College is to advance California's economic growth and global competencies through education, training, and services." CCIE played a leadership role on the 1999 State Chancellor's Office California Global Task Force. The resulting "vision" remains a guiding force in internationalization at California community colleges today.

One example of a cross-sector interinstitutional activity was the UCLA Teacher Training International Summer Institutes. CCIE helped create the community college emphasis for these programs, and from 1991–1995 over 75 faculty from 22 colleges participated. These faculty internationalized their classes and helped broaden education for their students. Many of these faculty subsequently participated in other international education programs on their campuses, which focused on leading study abroad programs, designing new academic programs, and participating in faculty exchange programs. Finally, a few of the faculty became senior administrators and kept their support for internationalization as part of their personal philosophy.

California hosts three specific cross-sector interinstitutional associations whose mission is to advance international education. The Southern California Consortium on International Studies (SOCCIS, 2013) is a voluntary association of public and private colleges and universities established in 1972 for the purpose of coordinating and sharing resources to further international studies and internationalization of the curriculum in the southern California region. The Northern California Advocates for Global Education was developed in 1990 to create a similar group in the northern California area. Another association, the California Council for Study Abroad (CalAbroad, 2013) is a collaborative of the UC system, the CSU system, and private universities and community colleges to promote study abroad.

Recommendations

CCIE recommends ways in which faculty, administrators, and other campus leaders can advocate international education.

1. Create a vision. International education should be part of any college mission and strategic plan, and it should involve the president, senior administrators, faculty, and staff.
2. Implement internationalization in creative ways. Study abroad programs are effective, but faculty can advance student global proficiencies by offering courses containing international themes and promoting foreign language courses. Infusing general education-based global proficiencies into courses is another way to expand student exposure to global topics.
3. Strengthen opportunities for student travel abroad by soliciting funding from college foundations and trustees, and members of local communities.

Conclusion

Collaboration is critical to initiating, building, and sustaining international education in community colleges. CCIE and other national associations have worked together to advocate global education for more than three decades. Yet internationalization is still not part of contemporary discourse for community college leadership training (Raby, 2007), nor for college level action items (Harder, 2011). Moreover, Green, Luu, and Burris (2008) show that international education is still a peripheral activity for community colleges, and Harder (2011) notes that in particular, rural community colleges have significantly less internationalization than their urban and suburban counterparts.

We argue that when international education remains on the sidelines, it is neither due to a budget crisis nor due to a lack of inclusion in mission. Periphery status has to do with the insularity upon which international education is built. This is an area where collaboration still needs to make an imprint.

California community college internationalization began and largely continues as a singular effort, usually by one faculty or one administrator on a college campus. Sometimes this exists in isolation because few on campus share similar enthusiasm for internationalization. Other times, a silo effect results when some international programs gain a profit margin, and efforts to remain separate results in political and budgetary rivalry. For example, study abroad programs often have different directors, budgets, and advocates than international student or international business programs. The detachment of offices contributes to a lack of campus visibility and diminished role in campus politics (Raby, 1999, 2007). Thus, it is common for education abroad programs to have different directors, and elements needed to build a comprehensive construct are often missing. The dissonance that frames international education directly relates to problems in how these programs establish themselves within the academic milieus.

Throughout the decades, collaboration has strongly shaped the importance and role of international education. Today, all community college associations have policy documents that support internationalization and philosophically "it is hard to find an American community college, [four-year] college, or university that has not devoted serious new thought, in recent years, to some aspect—often, to many aspects—of global education" (Stearns, 2009, p. 1). Nonetheless, the peripheral status of international education at community colleges, in California and nationally, has not changed much in the past three decades. Ironically, as students and the disciplines they study become more internationalized, and workforces that students will eventually enter value globalization, the community college appears to be going in the opposite direction. California Colleges for International Education (CCIE) is one of many consortia that continue to work to elicit institutional and academic change that will in turn support open access and the benefits of a higher education for all students. We conclude that colleges seeking to internationalize their programs adopt cornerstones that include collaboration across all units, organizational structures that are linked by specific goals and expectations, and measurement to assess effectiveness and communication strategies that identify success related to student access success and growth.

References

American Association of Community Colleges (AACC). (2012, April). *Reclaiming the American dream: A report from the 21st-century commission on the future of community colleges.* Washington, DC: Author. Retrieved from http://www.aacc.nche.edu /21stCenturyReport

California Colleges for International Education (CCIE). (2010). *Annual report.* Retrieved from http://www.ccieworld.org/reports.htm

California Colleges for International Education (CCIE). (2013). *Homepage.* Retrieved from http://www.ccieworld.org

California Council for Study Abroad (CalAbroad). (2013). *Homepage.* Retrieved from http://calabroad.org/

California Education Code Sec. 297 66010.4.3. (1999–2008). *California legislative information.* Retrieved from http://www.leginfo.ca.gov/cgi-bin/displaycode?section=edc& group=66001-67000&file=66010.1-66010.8

Green, M., Luu, D., & Burris, B. (Eds.). (2008). *Mapping internationalization on U.S. campuses.* Washington, DC: American Council on Education.

Harder, N. J. (2011). Internationalization efforts in United States community colleges: A comparative analysis of urban, suburban, and rural institutions. *Community College Journal of Research and Practice, 35*(1–2), 152–164.

Hess, G. (1982). *Freshmen and sophomores abroad: Community colleges and overseas academic programs.* New York, NY: Teachers College Press.

NAFSA: Association of International Educators and Institute for International Education (NAFSA/IIE). (2013). *International student economic value tool.* Retrieved from http://www.nafsa.org/Explore_International_Education/Impact/Data_And_Statistics/The _International_Student_Economic_Value_Tool/.

Raby, R. L. (1999). *Looking to the future: Report on international and global education in California community colleges.* Sacramento: State Chancellor, California Community Colleges Press.

Raby, R. L. (2007). Internationalizing the curriculum: On- and off-campus strategies. In E. J. Valeau & R. L. Raby (Eds.), *New Directions for Community Colleges: No. 138. International reform efforts and challenges in community colleges* (pp. 57–66). San Francisco, CA: Jossey-Bass.

Raby, R. L., Kaufman, J. P., & Rabb, G. (2012). The international negotiation modules project: Using simulation to enhance teaching and learning strategies in the community college. In R. Clothey, S. Austin-Li, & J. Weidman (Eds.), *Post-secondary education and technology: A global perspective on opportunities and obstacles to development* (pp. 181–201). New York, NY: Palgrave MacMillan.

Raby, R. L., & Valeau, E. J. (2007). Community college international education: Looking back to forecast the future. In E. J. Valeau & R. L. Raby (Eds.), *New Directions for Community Colleges: No. 138. International reform efforts and challenges in community colleges* (pp. 5–14). San Francisco, CA: Jossey-Bass.

Southern California Consortium on International Studies (SOCCIS). (2013). *Homepage.* Retrieved from http://soccis.org/

Stearns, P. N. (2009). *Educating global citizens in colleges and universities: Challenges and opportunities*. New York, NY: Routledge.

Zook, G. (1947). *The President's commission on higher education: Higher education for American democracy: Vol. 1. Establishing goals*. New York, NY: Harper & Brothers.

ROSALIND LATINER RABY *is a senior lecturer in the Educational Leadership and Policy Studies Department of the College of Education at California State University, Northridge. She is also the director of California Colleges for International Education.*

DONALD R. CULTON *is the retired director of Institute for International Education at the Los Angeles Community College District.*

EDWARD J. VALEAU *is president emeritus of Hartnell Community College. He is also president emeritus of California Colleges for International Education.*

9

This chapter describes the characteristics of successful partnerships between a state-level department and local community colleges. Particular focus is paid to the lack of mandated collaboration between the entities and the elements necessary for motivation and sustainability.

Collaborations Between the State and Local Colleges: Sleeping With the Enemy?

Elizabeth Cox Brand

In this era of diminishing resources and growing demand for accountability and results, collaboration between those with like interests has become more important, even critical to the success of an organization. The dictionary assigns two very different meanings to the term "collaborate." The most familiar is "to work with another person or group in order to achieve or do something." The other may be closer to the mindset of community colleges when asked to collaborate with a state-level agency or coordinating body: "to give help to an enemy who has invaded your country during a war" (Merriam-Webster, 2013).

This chapter will discuss the collaborative relationship between a state-level department and community colleges in Oregon, where the department has no governing authority, as in a system, to require that collaboration exists. Recommendations for the establishment of state and local collaborations will also be provided.

Introduction

Oregon community colleges were established in 1949 when the state legislature authorized school districts to create centers that provided college-level courses. Until the economic downturn of the 1980s, Oregon community colleges were strongly independent, having resisted the establishment of a strong coordinating agency at the state government level. During that decade and the financial crisis it brought, however, the colleges reassessed their opposition and obtained legislative approval to establish the Office of Community College Services. The bill was modified in 1997 to incorporate

NEW DIRECTIONS FOR COMMUNITY COLLEGES, no. 165, Spring 2014 © 2014 Wiley Periodicals, Inc.
Published online in Wiley Online Library (wileyonlinelibrary.com) • DOI: 10.1002/cc.20094

workforce programs, and the agency was renamed the Oregon Department of Community Colleges and Workforce Development (CCWD). Yet even with the creation of the department, Oregon community colleges remain largely independent, with no formal state system of governance in place. CCWD was a collaborative effort between colleges and workforce, state and local. Although CCWD does not have governing authority, it serves Oregon's community colleges through a variety of operations, including: the distribution of state funding to individual campuses; course and program approval; General Educational Development (GED) management; administration of federal funds, such as the Carl Perkins and Workforce Investment Act; and other critical functions. Through its very structure, CCWD exists as a collaborative effort between colleges and workforce, state and local.

Collaboration and Its Importance to Community Colleges

As pointed out above, the term "collaboration" can have different meanings, often based on the perception and experience one has had with past projects. Mattessich and Monsey (1992) define collaboration as "a mutually beneficial and well-defined relationship entered into by two or more organizations to achieve common goals" (p. 7). A further reading of the definition put forward by Mattessich and Monsey accurately portrays the nature of these agreements as complex and powerful, yet often very fragile.

Eddy (2010), in her book *Partnerships and Collaborations in Higher Education*, proposes that "partnerships are considered a collaborative between two or more institutions of higher education, businesses, or social agencies, with the goal of obtaining a shared objective" (p. 10). Since this definition more accurately describes the type of collaboration referred to in this article, partnerships will be used as the descriptive word for the relationship between the state and local colleges. Eddy further describes a critical component of partnerships as the notion that individual actors cannot accomplish the outcome alone, thus "the partnership creates the ultimate win-win situation" (p. 2).

The recession of the late 2000s brought about significant budget cuts for community colleges in Oregon, with funding declining by more than $100 million compared with a decade earlier. Although service to a community and region is central to the mission and DNA of the community college, institutions were forced to cut programs and reduce offerings, intensifying the impact of the recession in many areas of the state. The economic impact served as an incentive for both local colleges and the state to partner as policymakers, as they realized the importance of community colleges not only as providers of academic programs but also as an economic engine for the state. As Boehmer (2013) states, "What makes community colleges vital to regional success goes beyond individual students: our mission also calls upon us to build long-term strategic partnerships..." (para. 2).

Collaborating was also highlighted in *Reclaiming the American Dream*, a report from the American Association of Community Colleges (2012). It described "three R's" for restructuring community colleges, including the reinvention of institutional roles by way of "invest[ing] in support structures to serve multiple community colleges through collaboration among institutions and with partners in philanthropy, government, and the private sector" (p. x). Clearly, partnerships are viewed as critical to the vitality of community colleges in the 21st century. Partnerships are also an essential component for the state when resources are limited, the economy is stagnant, and accountability in the allotment of taxpayer dollars is demanded.

Motivations for Partnering

There are several reasons for and benefits of partnerships. Many have explored partnerships in higher education (Highman & Yeomans, 2010; Williams et al., 2011) and what makes for successful collaborations (Amey, Eddy, Campbell, & Watson, 2008; Mattessich & Monsey, 1992). Eddy (2010) outlined seven motivations for creating educational partnerships, including: education reform, economic development, dual enrollment or student transfer, student learning, resource savings, shared goals and visions, and international joint ventures (p. 3). This portion of the chapter will focus on six of those points as they pertain to Oregon community colleges; international joint ventures, as they are outside the scope of partnerships between the state and its community colleges, will not be addressed here.

The Oregon Context and Motivation

Like other states, Oregon has undertaken significant education reform. In 2011, the state legislature passed a law giving the state the highest education-attainment goals in the nation. The target: By 2025, 20% of residents would have a minimum of a high school diploma or equivalent, 40% a minimum of a certificate or associate's degree, and the remaining 40% a bachelor's degree or higher. This statute, commonly termed "40–40–20," continues to shape the state's education policy and practice.

A key component of this reform was the creation of the Oregon Educational Investment Board (OEIB). The board, appointed by Oregon's governor, was established to oversee a seamless pre-kindergarten-through-graduate-school (P–20) continuum. One of the first items of business for the board was the implementation of achievement compacts. Each segment had its own outcome metrics and targets approved by the OEIB, making for a compact between the state (OEIB) and the educational institution. While there currently are no repercussions for an institution that does not achieve its goals or targets, discussions of impending outcomes-based funding models are looming, and penalties may be on the horizon.

As a counter to the OEIB, legislation was also passed creating the Higher Education Coordinating Commission (HECC). This committee, also appointed by the governor, would have similar duties to the OEIB, except its focus would be exclusively on postsecondary education. As this chapter is being written, the HECC is being restructured. Legislation passed during the 2013 session gave the commission more authority, and all but two original members were replaced.

In the 2011 session in which "40–40–20" was passed, policymakers also established the Task Force on Higher Education Student and Institutional Success. The 17-member group, made up of representatives of CCWD, the Oregon University System Office of the Chancellor, and community college and university faculty and students, met over a six-month period to address issues including student debt and student transfer, and to examine best practices in the promotion of academic progression and completion. A report was presented to the state legislature that also led to the creation of additional groups to examine issues impacting student success, among them, the cost of textbooks and the role of credit for prior learning. Education reform clearly is top of mind in Oregon and promises to remain so for the foreseeable future.

All this reform was happening against the backdrop of the deepest recession the United States had experienced since the 1920s. State coffers were depleted due to lost tax revenues, education budgets were slashed, and unemployment in several areas of Oregon was the highest it had been in decades. As happens when the economy turns south, the community college becomes a focus. Dislocated workers and students flocked to community colleges for training and lower division collegiate courses. Oregon's community colleges saw record enrollment, which remains at a historically high level.

This combination of sweeping educational reform and economic recession encompassed several of the motivating factors outlined by Eddy (2010), including: education reform, in the form of legislation and the creation of governing boards and commissions; economic development, as community colleges were asked to step up and lead regional workforce and employment revival; dual enrollment or student transfer, specifically addressed in the achievement compacts; student learning, as the focus of other legislative action; resource savings, a high priority, as budgets were significantly cut; and shared goals and visions, between the state and local colleges, specifically as they pertain to students' academic success. Clearly, opportunity for partnerships between the state-level department and local community colleges was tremendous. Yet how would this manifest in an environment of fiercely independent colleges and a state agency that had no governing authority to mandate such partnerships?

Partnerships Between the State and Local Levels

It may seem that the lack of authoritative control at the state level would make the establishment and sustainability of such partnerships untenable. However, Dallmer (2004) found that consensus building to reach partnership goals is more effective than a mandated, top-down approach. Eddy (2010) echoed this, stating: "If institutions are mandated to collaborate, partners may not bring much intrinsic motivation to the effort or high level of trust for their collaborators. On the other hand, if a partnership forms based on mutual interests or shared goals, higher levels of intrinsic motivation are present and a different context exists for the partnership to operate" (p. 18). Clearly, mandating partnerships and collaborations does not mean they will be successful, much less sustainable. Instead, elements that lead to promising partnerships include shared goals, relationships with partners, leadership, and trustworthiness (Eddy, 2010). Collaborations that revolve around stakeholder values and goals are what Highman and Yeomans (2010) refer to as "committed collaborations." According to their study, "Committed collaboration[s] seemed more likely to be sustained, whereas technical and instrumental collaboration might collapse once contractual responsibilities lapse or funding ends" (p. 390).

Leadership also plays a crucial role in defining and driving partnerships. A key element of that leadership is the social capital the leader, or champion, has accrued. This social capital and the availability of organizational resources and assets are two central elements of influence in partnerships (Eddy, 2010). In particular, Eddy found that "...who the champion is matters to the partnership" (p. 34). In the case of Oregon's community colleges, the unifying champion for pursuing, solidifying, and sustaining partnerships between the state and local levels was the commissioner of CCWD.

Given the political frame in which the state agency resides, the leader of that department who has developed social capital, strong interpersonal relationships, and trustworthiness with individual college presidents, boards of trustees, governing boards, and legislators is in a prime position to successfully champion partnerships. Add to that access to a pool of state strategic funds to be distributed to local colleges, and the stage for partnerships is set. Fortunately for Oregon community colleges, the champion during this period of reform possessed all those characteristics.

A prime example of a successful partnership between the state and local levels was a committee formed by the champion to address various aspects of student success in community colleges. The Student Success Oversight Committee (SSOC) was designed to have input from various stakeholder groups for Oregon community colleges (e.g., the Council of Instructional Administrators and the Adult Basic Skills Directors), with each group selecting its own volunteer representatives to the committee. This committee has embodied many of the motivations for partnering, including shared goals, student learning, and dual enrollment or student transfer. In fact, one of the main outcomes of this group was a report outlining the academic progression and completion agenda for Oregon community colleges. Given the involvement of the commissioner, this committee was able to influence the potential investment of state strategic funds to support that agenda. This committee has been actively sustained since 2008, due to the presence of a strong champion and all the motivating factors for partnership.

Conclusion and Recommendations

Oregon is a state where one can experience higher education that is greatly centralized and governed, as in the Oregon University System, as well as a loosely coupled confederation of institutions whose success is largely dependent on collaboration and partnership, as is the case with its community colleges. Opportunities to compare and contrast the success of mandated, systematized partnerships and voluntary collaborations abound.

As noted here, several factors may influence the success and sustainability of partnerships. The following are offered as recommendations for the development of successful partnerships between the state and local levels:

- Identify an engaged leader who has the qualities to be a strong champion for the partnership. The history of relationships one has had with individual partners may influence success of the venture so should also be considered when selecting a champion.
- Emphasize shared visions and objectives of the partnership. Motivating factors for entering into a partnership may differ, but the closer the alignment of visions and objectives, the more likely a partnership will be successful and sustainable.
- Ensure the partnership has an appropriate cross-section of members. The partnership should ideally have college students, college presidents, academic administrators, and student affairs professionals.
- Involve leaders from business and industry, and education in the creation of state or regional goals that are concrete and attainable. In order to achieve buy-in and full support across the partnership, members must feel that the objectives for the collaboration are clear and realistic.

References

American Association of Community Colleges. (2012, April). *Reclaiming the American dream: A report from the 21st-century commission on the future of community colleges.* Washington, DC: Author. Retrieved from http://www.aacc.nche.edu/21stCenturyReport

Amey, M. J., Eddy, P. L., Campbell, T., & Watson, J. (2008, April). *The role of social capital in facilitating partnerships.* Paper presented at the 2008 Council for the Study of Community Colleges annual conference, Philadelphia, PA.

Boehmer, J. (2013). Let your partnerships prove your relevance. *Community College Times*. Retrieved from http://www.communitycollegetimes.com/Pages/Campus-Issues/Let-your-partnerships-prove-your-relevance.aspx

Dallmer, D. (2004). Collaborative relationships in teacher education: A personal narrative of conflicting roles. *Curriculum Inquiry, 34*(1), 29–45.

Eddy, P. L. (2010). *Partnerships and collaborations in higher education.* San Francisco, CA: Jossey-Bass.

Highman, J., & Yeomans, D. (2010). Working together? Partnership approaches to 14–19 education in England. *British Educational Research Journal, 36*(3), 379–401.

Mattessich, P. W., & Monsey, B. R. (1992). *Collaboration: What makes it work.* Saint Paul, MN: Wilder Research Center.

Merriam-Webster. (2013). *Collaborate.* Retrieved from http://www.merriam-webster.com/dictionary/collaborate

Williams, J. E., Wake, C., Hayden, L., Abrams, E., Hurtt, G., Rock, G., ... Johnson, D. (2011). Building a model of collaboration between historically black and historically white universities. *Journal of Higher Education Outreach and Engagement, 15*(2), 35–55.

ELIZABETH COX BRAND *is the director of Research and Communications for the Oregon Department of Community Colleges and Workforce Development.*

INDEX

AAC&U. *See* American Association for Colleges and Universities (AAC&U)

Abrams, E., 89

A Crucible Moment: College Learning and Democracy's Future, 37–38

Admissions pipeline, 61–62

Alavi, M., 50, 51, 53

Alfred, R., 27

American Association for Colleges and Universities (AAC&U), 30, 37

American Association of Community Colleges, 88

Amey, M. J., 9, 10, 89

Ash, S. L., 38

Azevedo, A., 60

Barbatis, P. R., 3, 59, 65

Barnett, E. A., 10, 30

Bashford, J., 28

Battistoni, R. M., 40

BCC. *See* Bronx Community College (BCC)

BCC Internship Coordinator, 42

BCTC. *See* Bluegrass Community and Technical College (BCTC)

Beebe, J., 11

Belfield, C., 27, 29

Bioland, P. A., 59

Bissonette, B., 68, 72

Bivens, G. M., 17, 22

Blankenship, P., 10

Bluegrass. *See* Opportunity Middle College (Bluegrass)

Bluegrass Community and Technical College (BCTC), 7

Blumenfeld, W. J., 17

Boehmer, J., 88

Bolt, W., 10, 44

Bragg, D. D., 10

Brand, E. C., 87, 92

Brandenberger, J., 38, 40, 41

Brennan, M., 70

Bringle, R., 40

Bronx Community College (BCC), 25, 38; Criminal Justice Program, 26–33, 42; dual enrollment at, 27; internship program of, 39–45; partnership with JJC, 32–33

Burke, J. C., 26

Burris, B., 68, 83

California Colleges for International Education (CCIE), 3, 69, 77–83

California Council for Study Abroad (CalAbroad), 82

Campbell, T. G., 9, 89

Carl Perkins and Workforce Investment Act, 88

CCID. *See* Community Colleges for International Development (CCID)

CCIE. *See* California Colleges for International Education (CCIE)

Center for Internationalization and Global Engagement (CIGE), 68

Chu, W. K., 52, 53

CIGE. *See* Center for Internationalization and Global Engagement (CIGE)

City University of New York (CUNY), 25

Civic identity, 39

Civic learning, 37–38

Clark, N., 73

Clayton, P. H., 38, 40, 42

Collaboration, 25–34, 77–84; with academic departments, 28–29; for advocacy, 78–80; on cross-sector statewide institutional projects, 81–82; definition of, 87, 88; grant proposal for, 26–27; with high schools, 27–28; importance to community colleges, 88–89; for international education, 77–78; International Negotiations Modules Project, 81; for programmatic and institutional change, 80–81; with Student Affairs, 31–32; with Office of Institutional Research, 31–32

Commonwealth Middle College (West Kentucky), 8–15. *See also* Middle College High School (MCHS)

Community College Journal of Research and Practice, 43

Community College National Council on Civic Engagement, 40

Community colleges, 18; importance of collaboration to, 88–89; international education programs, 77; opportunity

for high school students, 19; recommendations for, 21–22; rural, 17
Community Colleges for International Development (CCID), 68, 69
Core Indicators of Effectiveness for Community Colleges, 27
Creswell, J. W., 10
Criminal Justice Program (CRJ) at Bronx Community College, 26–33; internship program, 41
Cross-sector interinstitutional associations, 81–82
Culton, D. R., 3, 77, 85
Cunningham, C. L., 10
CUNY. *See* City University of New York (CUNY)
Customized educational plan, 63

Data-information-knowledge continuum, 56
Diverse life experience, of students, 38
Dellow, D. A., 70
DePaola, T., 2, 37, 46
Dewey, J., 38
Drumm, K. E., 5, 6
Dual-credit programs, 7
Dual enrollment programs, 27

Ebie, G., 38
Eddy, P. L., 9, 10, 88, 89
Educational partnerships, 9–10; of Academic Affairs and Student Affairs, 30–31; of John Jay College and Bronx Community College, 32–33; and Kentucky Middle College High Schools, 9–10; leadership in, 10, 91; motivations for, 89–92; P–12 and postsecondary education institutions, 9–14; physical space and, 19–20; promising practices in, 15; recommendations for, 92; between state and local levels, 90–92
Educause, 60, 64
Ewell, P., 27, 30
Experience and Education, 38

Farago, P., 62
First-Year Program (FYP), 55–57
Fitch, P., 41
Foley, D. J., 18
Fong, K., 28
Framework for Comprehensive Internationalization, 68
Freire, P., 41

Freshman Seminar (FYP), 29, 30
FYP. *See* First-Year Program (FYP)

Gazely, B., 40
Gildersleeve, R. E., 17
Gosetti, P. P., 3, 67, 74
Graham, K., 89
Grant proposals, 26–28; BCC and JJC partnership for, 25; designing, 26–27; recommendations for, 33–34
Green, M., 68, 70, 83

Hagedorn, L. S., 31, 67
Harbour, C. P., 38
Harder, N., 73, 83
Hardiman, R., 38
Hardy, D. E., 17
Harris-Hardland, G., 28
Hayden, L., 89
HECC. *See* Higher Education Coordinating Commission (HECC)
Hess, G. R., 42, 80
Higher Education Coordinating Commission (HECC), 90
Highman, J., 89
Hill, B., 68, 70
Hizmetli, H., 2, 3, 49, 52, 58
Hudgins, J., 27
Hudson, T., 41
Hudzik, J. K., 68, 70, 72, 73
Hughes, K. L., 27, 29
Hurst, J. C., 59
Hurtt, G., 89
Hyman, R., 59

INMP. *See* International Negotiations Modules Project (INMP)
Inside Rikers: Stories for the World's Largest Penal Colony, 28
Institutional partnerships. *See* Educational partnerships
International education, 77–84; advocacy, 78–80; background of, 78; cross-sector statewide institutional projects, 81–82; programmatic and institutional change, 80–81; recommendations for, 82
Internationalization, in community colleges, 67–74; challenges to, 72–73; chief academic officer role in supporting, 69–72; chief executive officer role in supporting, 69–71; chief international officer role in supporting, 70; chief student affairs officer role in

supporting, 69–72; comprehensive, 68; current status of, 68–69; facilitators of, 71–72; key administrators supporting, 69–70; overview, 67; reasons for, 70–71
International Negotiations Modules Project (INMP), 80

Jackson, B. W., 38
Jackson, K. L., 9, 10
Jacoby, B., 40, 41
Jaeger, A. J., 42
Jameson, J. K., 38, 42
Jarsky, K. M., 17
JJC. *See* John Jay College of Criminal Justice (JJC)
John Jay College of Criminal Justice (JJC), 25; admissions policy of, 25–26; partnering with Bronx Community College, 32–33
Johnson, D., 89
Johnson, L., 60
Johnston, G., 31
Joint Statement on the Role of Community Colleges in International Education, 67

Karp, M. M., 27
Katsinas, S. G., 17
Kaufman, J. P., 81
KCTCS. *See* Kentucky Community and Technical College System (KCTCS)
Kentucky Community and Technical College System (KCTCS), 7
Kentucky Postsecondary Education Improvement Act, 7
Kiernan, V., 60, 61, 64
Kim, E., 10
Kirkwood Community College, 73
KMS. *See* Knowledge management systems (KMS)
Knowledge base indicators, in information systems, 53–54
Knowledge management (KM) practices, 49–58; converting data into information, 52–53; establishing FYP, 54–55; establishing IT infrastructure, 52; integrating knowledge base indicators in information systems, 53–54; knowledge base about student success, 53; phases for implementation of, 51–55; recommendations for, 57–

58; theory of, 50–51; through collaboration, 55–57
Knowledge management systems (KMS), 50
Kress, A. M., 31
Kuh, G. D., 59

Largent, L., 42, 43
Latina students, rural, 18–19; community colleges for, 18; counselor for, 20–22; family and community support to, 22; participating in STEM activities, 19
Lau, L., 63
Leadership, role in partnership, 91
LEAP. *See* Liberal Education and America's Promise (LEAP)
Lebovitz, A., 28
Legasa, F., 56
Leidner, D. E., 50, 51, 53, 57
Levi, A. J., 30
Levin, J., 45
LGBTQ advocacy, 43
LGBTQ discrimination, 43
Liberal Education and America's Promise (LEAP), 37
Lillibridge, F., 31
Littlepage, L., 40
Luu, D. T., 68, 83

Maki, P., 30
Mapping Internationalization on U.S. Campuses, 68, 72
Marcus, J., 60
Massively Open Online Course (MOOC) consortium, 60
Mattessich, P. W., 10, 88, 89
Mayo, T., 10
McCarthy, J. S., 68, 70, 72, 73
McClenny, K., 27
McDonough, P., 17
McGuire, L. E., 42
MCHS. *See* Middle College High School (MCHS)
Middle College High School (MCHS), 7; educational partnerships, 9–10; findings on, 12–14; research methods to study, 10–12
Minnassians, H., 26
Mobelini, D. C., 32
Monsey, B. R., 10, 88, 89
Mooney, G. M., 18
Murray-Close, M., 10

New Directions for Community Colleges, 5, 67
Nodine, T. R., 49, 50, 51, 54

OEIB. *See* Oregon Educational Investment Board (OEIB)
Office of Institutional Research, collaboration with, 31–32
Opp, R. D., 3, 67, 74
Opportunity Middle College (Bluegrass), 7–15. *See also* Middle College High School (MCHS)
Oregon community colleges, 87–92; Department of Community Colleges and Workforce Development, 88; education reform in, 89–90; motivations for partnership, 89–90; Oregon Educational Investment Board, 89–90; overview, 87–88; state and local level partnership, 90–92
Oregon Educational Investment Board (OEIB), 89
OSSESS, 52
Ozaki, C. C., 10

Partnerships and Collaborations in Higher Education, 88
Pedagogy of the Oppressed, 41
Petrides, L. A., 49, 50, 51, 54
Philpott, J. L., 31
Physical space, 19–20; to build educational partnerships, 19–20; within educational communities, 21
PLTW. *See* Project Lead the Way (PLTW)
Prentice, M., 40
Program objective course compliance, 63–64
Project Lead the Way (PLTW), 18–21
Pusser, B., 45

Rabb, G., 81
Raby, R. L., 3, 67, 77, 78, 79, 81, 83, 84
RAP. *See* Rapid Assessment Process (RAP)
Rapid Assessment Process (RAP), 11
Reclaiming the American Dream, 78, 88
Report from the President's Commission on Higher Education, 78
Ritze, N., 52, 54, 56
Robinson, G., 40
Rock, G., 89

Rodriguez, O., 27, 29
Rogers, R. R., 59
Roggow, M. J., 4, 25, 34
Ruiz, E., 52, 54
Rural communities, 17–18

Schroeder, C. S., 59
Sedziuviene, N., 50
Service learning, 38–39
Sink, D. W., Jr., 9, 10
Smart-device applications, 62–63; challenges during peak registration periods, 63; customized educational plan, 63; develop relationships with, 62; GPS, 62
SOCCIS. *See* Southern California Consortium on International Studies (SOCCIS)
Social inequality, 38
Social justice, through service learning, 37–46
Southern California Consortium on International Studies (SOCCIS), 82
SSOC. *See* Student Success Oversight Committee (SSOC)
Stamatakos, L. C., 59
Starobin, S. S., 17, 22
State University of New York's Broome Community College (SUNY Broome), 5
Stearns, P. N., 83
Steinke, P., 41
Stephenson, L. G., 1, 7, 10
Stevens, D. D., 30
Student affairs and information technology, partnership of, 59–65; admissions pipeline, 61–62; customized educational plan, 63; emerging and promising practices of, 61–64; financial aid program objective course compliance, 63–64; needs analysis of, 60–61; overview, 59–60; recommendations for, 64; smart-device applications, 62–63; technological advances and, 60
Student reflection, 42
Student Success Oversight Committee (SSOC), 91
Summer Bridge Program, 32
SUNY Broome. *See* State University of New York's Broome Community College (SUNY Broome)

Support Education Excellence in Kentucky (SEEK) funding, 8, 9

Task Force on Higher Education Student and Institutional Success, 90
Tinto, V., 30
Treat, T., 67
Tsapogas, J., 18

Valeau, E. J., 3, 67, 77, 85
Vveinhardt, J., 50

Wach, H., 56
Wagonlander, C. S., 10
Wake, C., 89
Wang, M., 52, 53
Watson, J., 89

West Kentucky. See Commonwealth Middle College (West Kentucky)
West Kentucky Community and Technical College (WKCTC), 8
Williams, J. E., 89
Willis, J., 19
WKCTC. See West Kentucky Community and Technical College (WKCTC)
Woodin, S., 68, 72
Wynn, J., 28

Yeomans, D., 89
Young, J. R., 60
Yuen, A. H., 52, 53

Zook, G., 78